SCIENCE 810

W9-AVA-128

Science and Technology

LIFEPAC Test is located in the center of the booklet. Please remove before starting the unit.

Author:
Hilda Bruno, M.A.

Editor-in-Chief:
Richard W. Wheeler, M.A.Ed.
Editor:
Mary L. Meyer
Consulting Editor:
Harold Wengert, Ed.D.
Revision Editor:
Alan Christopherson, M.S.

Westover Studios Design Team:
Phillip Pettet, Creative Lead
Teresa Davis, DTP Lead
Nick Castro
Andi Graham
Jerry Wingo
Don Lechner

804 N. 2nd Ave. E.
Rock Rapids, IA 51246-1759

Science and Technology

Introduction

We are blessed with a natural curiosity that may lead us into strange places. This curiosity stimulates questions and a search for answers. When the study of natural and physical things in the world is conducted in an orderly fashion, we arrive at a scientific conclusion. When the conclusion is applied in a practical way, it is technology. In Science LIFEPACs 801 through 809, you have studied science and technology. These two areas are the basis for many types of jobs and gratifying careers.

Even before God closed off the garden of Eden, God told Adam and Eve to keep the garden; He told them to work. The Bible becomes even more emphatic about this instruction in 2 Thessalonians 3:10. The apostle Paul wrote to God's people, "...if any would not work, neither should he eat." God expects us to work, but He provides a reward if we work well. Jesus said in Luke 10:7 that "...the labourer is worthy of his hire."

You are old enough to think seriously about plans for your future. Ask God to open your eyes to all the possibilities and to guide you. In the next ten years, the number of people expected in the work force is greater than the number of jobs anticipated. Do you think you should quit school as soon as you can so you can jump into the competition for a job? Vocational analysis in government, industry, and labor say a loud "No." Employers are becoming more careful in their hiring practices. The better qualified applicant will get the job.

You have not had enough education or experience to decide on a vocation now. In this LIFEPAC®, we shall review the science you have studied, we shall consider technology, and we shall try to make personal career choices. Practical application of science principles will be made to help you. Ask God's help each time you open this LIFEPAC. He will guide your thinking and planning.

Objectives

Read these objectives. The objectives tell you what you will be able to do when you have successfully completed this LIFEPAC. When you have finished this LIFEPAC, you should be able to:

1. Compare science of the past to science of the present.
2. Explain the scientific method.
3. Calculate measurements in the metric system.
4. Describe the characteristics of matter and matter in change.
5. List examples of potential and kinetic energy and show work accomplished.
6. Explain the forms of conversion of energy.
7. Describe magnetism and its relation to electricity.
8. List vocations available in science and technology dependent on electricity.
9. Explain the meaning of work scientifically and in view of Christian responsibility.
10. List simple machines and explain each in terms of examples from daily life.
11. Explain how the human body functions like a machine.
12. Tell how we must care for our body as "the temple of God."
13. List job opportunities in the life sciences.
14. Describe the balance and disruptions of nature and state your place in the universe.
15. Describe vocational opportunities in science and technology.
16. Develop techniques for working out a career plan.

Survey the LIFEPAC. Ask yourself some questions about this study and write your questions here.

_____

_____

_____

_____

_____

_____

_____

_____

_____

_____

_____

_____

_____

_____

_____

_____

_____

_____

_____

1. BASIC SCIENCE

Vocations in science today require certain general skills. You must work according to the scientific method, record findings carefully and in order, and develop skill in mathematics and measurements.

Proficiency in general scientific skills is excellent, but it will not guarantee a job for you. You must develop two personal skills, **adaptability** and **resiliency**. If you are willing to accept circumstances and move along with good humor when things do not work out just as you desire, your chance for success is good. Putting road blocks in front of us is one way God directs us to do His will. He also wants us to be persevering and to stick with the task if we are convinced it is what God wants us to do.

The earth and all that is in it was created by God. To understand the world around us requires a basic understanding of the smallest particles of matter.

SECTION OBJECTIVES

Review these objectives. When you have completed this section, you should be able to:

1. Compare science of the past to science of the present.

2. Explain the scientific method.

3. Calculate measurements in the metric system.

4. Describe the characteristics of matter and matter in change.

VOCABULARY

Study these words to enhance your learning success of this section.

adaptability (u dap tu bil' u tē). Power to change easily to fit different conditions.

anthracite (an' thru sīt). A coal that burns with very little smoke or flame; hard coal.

bituminous (bu tü' mu nus). Coal that burns with much smoke and yellow flame; hard coal.

chemical formula (kem' u kul fôr' myü lu). An expression showing by symbols and figures the composition of a compound.

electrolysis (I lek trol' u sis). The decomposition of a chemical compound by the passage of an electrical current through a solution of the compound.

electroplate (I lek' tru plāt). To cover with a coating of metal by means of electrolysis.

experiment (ek sper' u munt). To try to find out; make trials; tests.

investigate (in ves' tu gāt). To search into; examine closely.

ion (ī un). An electrically charged particle.

isotope (ī' su top). Any of two or more forms of a chemical element having the same chemical properties and same atomic number but different atomic weights.

molecular structure (mu lek' yu lur struk' chur). Manner in which the atoms of a particular molecule are attached to one another.

obsolete (ob' su lāt). No longer in use; out-of-date.

proficiency (pru fish' un sē). Knowledge; skill, expertness.

prospective (pru spek' tiv). Looking forward to the future.

residue (rez' u dü). What remains after a part is taken; remainder.

resiliency (ri zil' e un sē). The power of springing back; buoyancy, cheerfulness.

structure (struk' chur). In chemistry the manner in which atoms making up a particular molecule are attached to one another.

subscript (sub' skript). Written underneath or low on the line.

Note: *All vocabulary words in this LIFEPAC appear in* **boldface** *print the first time they are used. If you are not sure of the meaning when you are reading, study the definitions given.*

Pronunciation Key: hat, āge, cãre, fär; let, ēqual, tėrm; it, īce; hot, ōpen, ôrder; oil; out; cup, pu̇t, rüle; child; long; thin; /ŦH/ for then; /zh/ for measure; /u/ or /ə/ represents /a/ in about, /e/ in taken, /i/ in pencil, /o/ in lemon, and /u/ in circus.

SCIENCE SKILLS

Aristotle is given credit for being the first to use an orderly system in his study of plants and animals. He did not **investigate** to see if his findings were true. Therefore, he is not thought of as a true scientist.

Meaning. Science comes from the Greek word meaning *to know* or *to discern. Discern* means *to perceive* and *to separate things out mentally. Perceive* means *to recognize differences by the senses.* With our minds and senses we must distinguish between facts. The meaning of *science* has changed through the years from its original Greek meaning of *to know* to *a systematized knowledge derived from observation, study, and experimentation.*

- **Observation**: the practice of noting and recording facts and events

- **Investigation**: a careful systematic search to learn facts

- **Experiment**: a test to discover something not yet known or demonstrate something known

The Scientific Method

Method. Since we have added to our original meaning of science, we must practice ways of developing systematized knowledge, recording observations, and experimentation. To know what we are doing, we must develop personal study skills. The scientific method is a skill the prospective scientist must master.

In Science LIFEPAC 801, you learned the nine steps of the scientific method:

1. choose a problem;
2. state what you think is the probable solution to the problem;
3. research what other scientists have done to solve the problem;
4. experiment to prove or disprove your hypothesis;
5. state the hypothesis again as a theory;
6. if wrong, state a new hypothesis;
7. write a paper on what you did to prove your hypothesis;
8. change your hypothesis if it is proved wrong;
9. state the theory as a law.

As a young scientist, you will not do all the steps of the scientific method, but you will have to practice how to observe, to investigate, and to **experiment**. A standard way of keeping records will help you to be accurate and complete. You will use the *Science Record*. Be sure to distinguish between an observation, an investigation, and an experiment.

Complete this activity.

1.1   List the nine steps of the scientific method in order.

a. _____   b. _____

c. _____   d. _____

e. _____   f. _____

g. _____   h. _____

i. _____

Match these items.

1.2   _____ heating ice to change to water and to steam

1.3   _____ noticing that the building is tall

1.4   _____ watching birds fly

1.5   _____ listing colors of birds in your back yard

1.6   _____ using a thermometer to find temperature of boiling water

1.7   _____ counting the people walking through the hallway

1.8   _____ using a crowbar to open a wooden box

a. observation

b. investigation

c. experimentation

Complete this investigation.

1.9 Complete the following Science Record (SR) by writing your name and the date.

a. Number the Science Record. Future Science Records will be numbered consecutively (2, 3, and so forth).

b. Place Statement 1 in the correct blank.

c. Place Statement 2 in the correct blank.

d. Place Statement 3 in the correct blank.

e. Place Statement 4 in the correct blank.

f. Write your own results based on the information given.

g. Write your own conclusion based on the information given.

Statements

1. Has science advanced since Aristotle? How?

2. Science LIFEPAC 801, an encyclopedia, or an online resource.

3. Read A BRIEF HISTORY OF SCIENCE from Science LIFEPAC 801 or an article about the history of science in an encyclopedia or online resource.

4. Many people contributed to the advancement of science.

SCIENCE RECORD

Observation # _____   Name _____

Investigation # _____   Date _____

Experiment # _____

Problem: _____

Materials: _____

Method: _____

Result: _____

_____

_____

_____

Conclusion: _____

_____

_____

_____

Measurement. The metric system is used by scientists all over the world. The modern metric system is known as the International System of Units. The name International System of Units with the international abbreviation SI was given to the system by the General Conference on Weights and Measures in 1960. Most countries except the United States, which still uses the English or customary system, have converted all measurements to metric units. Great Britain, from whom we got the English system, uses the metric system. Canada put metric measurements on the highway speed and distance signs in 1977.

Although President Ford signed the Metric Conversion Act in 1975 and in 1977 President Carter named the United States Metric Board to plan the voluntary conversion to metric. Ronald Reagan abolished the Metrication Board in 1982 and the United States has not completely converted to the metric system. However, all foreign countries use the metric system. Therefore, all industries making engines and other equipment made to be sold in foreign countries will use metric. Farmers, housewives, and everyone using things produced in foreign countries and the United States will need to know metric to use and repair these metric items. This international usage requires that everyone learns how to use the metric system.

Although the SI system has not been fully adopted in the U.S., it is commonly used in many places and we are more metric than most of us realize. Have you ever ran in a 100-meter dash, or a 5K or 10K race? The engine sizes for automobiles, motorcycles, recreational vehicles, and other small motors are given in cubic centimeters or liters. Mechanics have sets of wrenches in their tool boxes for both millimeter and inch sizes. Many beverage containers come in a metric size. The medical field and pharmaceuticals use metric units. The U.S. military is almost exclusively metric. Since 1994, many products have been required to include both metric and customary units by the Fair Label and Packaging Act. Just take a look at a box of breakfast cereal or a package of cookies and you will see both measurements. The electronics, chemical, and electric power industries have all adopted metrics at least in part, as have such fields as optometry and photography. Most rulers include both centimeters and inches as the common divisors. In school, both the metric and customary units are taught.

 Write the prefix to the word and the abbreviation in the blanks. You may review Science LIFEPAC 801 or consult an encyclopedia for this activity.

	Prefix			Abbreviation
1.10	_____	gram	= 1,000 grams	_____
1.11	_____	gram	= 100 grams	_____
1.12	_____	gram	= 10 grams	_____
1.13	_____	gram	= 1 gram	_____
1.14	_____	gram	= 0.1 gram	_____
1.15	_____	gram	= 0.01 gram	_____
1.16	_____	gram	= 0.001 gram	_____

Fluency with the metric system will be essential if you choose a career in science, technology, or many other fields.

The metric system is a preferred form of measurement because the units have a uniform scale of relationship–the decimal. The main units are the *meter* for length, *liter* for volume, and *kilogram* for mass. In metrics, temperature is measured in degrees *Celsius.* The thermometer is divided into 100 degrees from freezing (0) to boiling (100). The units of the metric system are consistent with multiples of ten and have uniform names.

 Complete this chart for the meter.

	Name		Number of Meters	Abbreviation
1.17		=		
1.18		=		
1.19		=		
	meter	=	1 meter	m
1.20		=		
1.21		=		
1.22		=		

Answer these questions.

1.23 List five places where metric units are commonly used in the U.S.

a. _____   b. _____

c. _____   d. _____

e. _____

1.24 What is the maximum speed limit in metric and English units?

a. _____   metric

b. _____   English

TEACHER CHECK _____ _____
　　　　　　　　　　　initials　　date

CHARACTERISTICS OF MATTER

John Dalton of England proposed his atomic theory in 1808. He thought the atom was like a saucer. Today, we know the electrons are whirling around the nucleus in different orbits at different levels. Understanding both the hugeness of the universe and the tiny details of the atom is a difficult task. God has written a mystery in the heavens and on earth that challenges our imagination and keeps us looking for answers to our questions. The orderliness of both the universe and the atom is an excellent example of pure science. Because of this orderliness, matter can be described and classified by its properties.

Properties of matter. Matter is a substance you can identify with your five senses. You test it for appearance, odor, touch, taste, mass, volume, and so forth. All materials have characteristics and can be recognized by these characteristics.

Human beings are constantly testing for the properties of matter. A baby reaches for an object; later the baby touches it; and then the baby recognizes color, shape, and form. Soon a child adds the use of other senses. Through observation, the child, and later the adult, learns that things have size, take up space, and have mass. The general characteristics of color, odor, taste, hardness, brittleness, luster, and form are observed. These characteristics are called the *physical properties of matter*.

Can you identify a rock by its physical characteristics? Select a specific rock specimen. Examine it. You may find it is not as hard as most rocks. Perhaps the rock is very black. Small chips fall off and seem to have a definite structure. Rubbing the rock makes your hands black. The peculiar odor is familiar to you. You decide it is coal. If you have had any experience with coal, you know it must be **bituminous**, or soft coal.

Anthracite, or hard coal, usually does not rub off on your hands easily. You have decided it is a solid and have, therefore, eliminated liquid or gas as a form. The piece of coal is part of a truckload of coal delivered for your fireplace. The half ton your father ordered takes up space and must be stored. The pile of coal has mass and volume. By finding the density of the coal with the formula *mass divided by volume*, you can learn another property. Compare the piece of coal to another rock of equal size, and you might be able to compare the density. A review of Science LIFEPAC 802 will give some help with this problem. If both rocks have a volume of 40 cm^3, the coal weighs 120 g, and the other rock weighs 160 g, which has the greater density?

To find the density of an unknown object, find the mass of the object first. Place a beaker or cup in another dish that can catch the overflow water. Fill the beaker or cup with water to the top. Drop your unknown object into the water and catch the overflow. Measure the overflow with the graduated cylinder. Remember, the curved surface of the liquid in a graduated cylinder is read at the bottom. How many cm^3 is it? Divide the mass in grams by the cm^3 and you will know the density of your object.

When the density of an object is less than the fluid it is floating in, the fluid beneath the object exerts an upward push or force called *buoyancy*. Density and buoyancy are special properties of matter.

Try this investigation.

These supplies are needed:

- 6 unidentified items in a box
- beaker or cup
- dish to catch water
- graduated cylinder, 10 ml, 25 ml, or 100 ml
- magnet
- balance, digital scale, or spring scale

Follow these directions. Put a check in the box when each step is completed.

☐ 1. Select a partner to work with you. Partner's name _____

☐ 2. Ask the teacher for the box of unknown items.

☐ 3. Use the Science Record form.

☐ 4. Number the SR form as Experiment #1.

☐ 5. Write the problem: How can unknown objects be identified by their physical properties?

☐ 6. Complete the SR form as you make tests on the unknown objects. Keep careful, accurate records. The six items in box should be tested by using the senses, finding the mass and density, observing magnetic properties, and so forth. A good attempt should be made to identify each object. Identification is good, but the manner of conducting the experiment and writing up the information is more important.

Physical Properties Experiment

SCIENCE RECORD

Observation # _____   Name _____

Investigation # _____   Date _____

Experiment # _____

Problem: _____

Materials: _____

Method: _____

Result: _____

_____

_____

_____

_____

_____

_____

_____

_____

_____

Conclusion: _____

_____

_____

_____

_____

_____

_____

_____

_____

TEACHER CHECK _____ _____

initials   date

Complete these sentences.

1.25 Paper and cork float on water because they have low _____ .

1.26 The water underneath the floating object exerts a push or force called _____ that holds it up.

1.27 The metric temperature scale is called _____ .

1.28 The curved surface of the liquid in a graduated cylinder is read at the _____ .

1.29 The characteristics of the properties of matter can be determined by _____

_____

_____

_____

Organization of matter. Water is the most plentiful substance on earth. The sea covers three-fourths of the earth. More water is trapped in glaciers and the icecaps of the North Pole and South Pole. The cause of water shortages has been the increased use of water by people and industry. We need to find ways to get water to the place *where* it is needed *when* it is needed.

Considering the amount of water on earth, a water shortage is difficult to understand. If you have a pail of water and pour it out until none is left in the pail you would say it is all gone. Although the pail seems to be empty, turn it upside down and a few more drops will run out. Now you are sure you have used the last particle of the water! Rub your finger over the inside surface of the pail and droplets of moisture cling to your finger. The pail will not be completely empty until the last *molecule* of water has been removed.

The molecule is the smallest particle of matter and its **structure** identifies the substance. We can split each molecule of water into separate elements, but then it is no longer water. By passing an electric current through water, two gases are formed. When the gases are collected and tested, they are found to be hydrogen and oxygen. This procedure verifies the **chemical formula** we use for water, H_2O. The amount of hydrogen collected is twice the amount of oxygen, as shown in the formula. Two atoms of hydrogen and one atom of oxygen are found in every molecule of water.

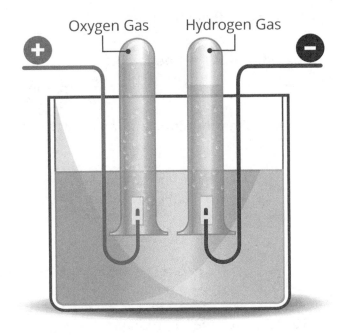

Figure 1 | Electrolysis of Water

In future scientific studies, you will probably do an experiment passing electric current through water. The positive **ions** are attracted to the negative pole, and the negative ions are attracted to the positive pole. The water molecules split into hydrogen and oxygen gases. Bubbles of the gases will collect in the test tubes (see Figure 1). This process is known as **electrolysis**.

A practical use of electrolysis is **electroplating**. The object to be plated is attached to the positive (see Figure 2). The solution is made up of metal. The electric current separates the metal of the solution and coats it on the item to be plated.

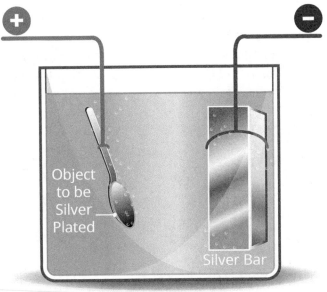

Figure 2 | Electroplating

Try this investigation.

These supplies are needed:

■ dish   ■ ammonia

Follow these directions and answer the questions. Put a check in the box when each step is completed.

☐ 1. Record the time as you place a dish in a draft-free corner of the room.
        Pour enough ammonia in the dish to cover just the bottom.
        Close the bottle of ammonia. Be sure no ammonia spills on your hands
        or clothes.

☐ 2. Move ten feet away from the dish. Record the time you begin to smell
        the ammonia.

1.30   Do you smell ammonia? _____

1.31   At what time did you smell the ammonia? _____

1.32   How long did it take to reach you? _____

OPTIONAL. Try this investigation at home with other liquids that have a strong odor, such as cleaning solutions, fingernail polish, spoiled eggs, and so forth. Try to find the speed the odor travels at different distances. Record the different times at different distances. No other computation is necessary. Write up each trial on a Science Record. Make your own form as you write up the trials using the divisions as given in the Science form. From now on, you will make your own Science Record forms.

TEACHER CHECK _____ _____
                                       initials   date

Diffusion Experiment

The traveling smell of the ammonia shows us that the molecules of the ammonia gas travel through the air and move between the air molecules that fill the room. Molecules of the air are different from the molecules of ammonia. They have different characteristics.

If you hit a nail with a hammer, the nail may bend or flatten, but it is still a nail. The flattened nail has the same **molecular structure** that it had before you struck it. The molecules have an attraction for each other that holds them together.

In such ways God provides the bonds that hold the universe in place.

We have learned four basic facts about matter:

1. Matter is made up of very small particles called molecules.

2. Each kind of matter has its own kind of molecules.

3. Molecules are in quick and perpetual motion.

4. Molecules attract each other.

 Match these items.

1.33	_____ keeps molecules together	a. atom
1.34	_____ small particle of matter	b. cubic centimeter
1.35	_____ unit of measure	c. electroplating
1.36	_____ break down water using electricity	d. theory
1.37	_____ measure amount of water	e. attraction
1.38	_____ practical use of electrolysis	f. molecule
1.39	_____ found in molecules	g. graduated cylinder
		h. electrolysis

The water molecule. During the process of water electrolysis, hydrogen and oxygen were obtained. The two gases separated. The individual gases are combustible if ignited and would explode. Water is a noncombustible substance used to put out fires. Therefore, we see that atoms have special characteristics that are not the same as the molecules in which they are found. After the explosion, we would find moisture. The water had reappeared.

The close partnership of atoms to form molecules is known as molecular structure. This structure is demonstrated in drawings or by making models as shown in Figure 3.

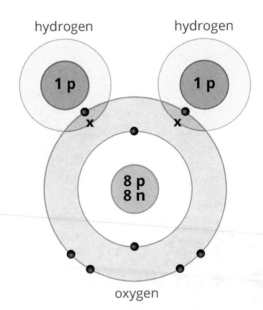

Figure 3 | Water Molecule

Complete these activities.

These supplies are needed:

- styrofoam balls (1 in. and 2 in.) (two of each)   ▪ pipe cleaners

Make models of water (H_2O), sand (SiO_2), and salt (NaCl) by connecting the styrofoam balls with pipe cleaners. Mark each ball with the symbol of the element it represents. The connection point of the ball and pipe cleaner represents the shared electrons. (Example: In CO_2 each oxygen atom shares two of carbon's electrons to complete the outer orbits.) After you have made the models, sketch them in the spaces.

1.40 water molecule

1.41 sand molecule

1.42 salt molecule

Molecular Structure Experiment

Discovering the atom. Greeks in about 400 B.C. identified what they thought was the smallest particle of matter. They called it the *atom,* which means *without a cutting*. The discoveries of the twentieth century have made great changes. Lord Ernest Rutherford in 1911 built the first model of the interior of the atom. It had a nucleus with electrons whirling about it. In 1913 Niels Bohr, a Danish chemist working in Rutherford's laboratory, found that the electrons keep certain paths or orbits around the nucleus. For this discovery he won the Nobel Prize in 1922. We have found more elements in recent years and talk about other particles discovered in the atom. *Positrons* are important in the theory of nuclear reactions and changing one element into another. *Mesons* were first discovered in cosmic rays and have since been produced artificially. *Neutrinos* are believed to account for certain nuclear reactions. *Deuteron* is the nucleus of heavy hydrogen and is used for bombarding nuclei. The new discoveries are but a part of what has been learned in recent years about the atom and molecule. Investigation continues. As you read this LIFEPAC, scientists are talking about atoms. New conclusions are being made that will make this information about atoms and molecules partially **obsolete**. Much of the push to accomplish this research has come from the study of *nuclear energy*. As scientists worked to release the energy from the atom, they discovered a great deal about the atom. These discoveries led to the first chain reaction in uranium and the release of energy that could be put to use. The program of research that led to this finding was designed to create an atomic bomb.

Discovering elements. The things about us are composed of *elements* in such a form that we can see them. Elements are substances that have only one kind of atom. Aristotle said matter was made of four elements, earth water, air, and fire. Today, we know that not one of the four is an element. They are compounds or mixtures. Ninety-two different kinds of atoms occur naturally and scientists have made even more. **Isotopes** of some elements have been observed; therefore, today we know of at least 109 elements. Although Aristotle was not correct, he led the world in its search for all the basic elements.

Elements exist in the three forms of matter: solid, liquid, or gas. You have probably used many elements, such as gold, silver, copper, oxygen, helium, mercury, and iodine. When two or more elements are joined together, they are called *compounds.* Since they are chemically joined together, they are difficult to separate. An element may be compared to a digit. The number of possible compounds would compare to the unbelievable number of possible combinations of the digits 0 to 9. The amount is beyond our understanding. More than 5 million compounds, formed from approximately one hundred elements, are now known to humans.

If the study of matter were to continue, a brief method of identifying the elements had to be found. The Greeks began by assigning symbols from Greek mythology to the elements. This method became too awkward, and the scientists had difficulty agreeing on what symbol to use. In 1814 a Swedish chemist named Berzelius began the system we have today. Frequently he used the first letter of the name of the element or the abbreviation from the Latin. Later, non-Latin words were used. To identify a compound, he combined the symbols of the atoms in the compounds. The **subscript** tells us how many atoms of that element are in the molecule of a compound. We call this notation a chemical formula. The use of symbols and chemical formulas has given science a special shorthand language of its own.

Complete these statements.

1.43 The Nobel Prize was won by a. _____ for finding that electrons in the atom stay in b. _____ .

1.44 Elements contain _____ of the same kind.

1.45 The shorthand of science is the use of _____ .

1.46 The new discoveries about the atom have been encouraged by the special study of

_____ .

1.47 In the formula $CaCO_3$ are a. _____ atom(s) of oxygen, b. _____ atom(s) of calcium, and c. _____ atom(s) of carbon.

Complete this activity.

1.48 Learn the symbols of the elements before you go on in your science studies. Use the Periodic Table of Elements. One is located in Science LIFEPAC 802. Have another student check your work. Explain the use of the Periodic Table to your teacher. Write here how many elements you have learned.

_____

TEACHER CHECK _____ _____

initials   date

Mixtures. Mixtures have been familiar to you all your life. Your dry baby food was mixed with water; later, you made mud pies, flour and water paste, and so on. Each mixture could be dried out and you were left with baby food, dirt, and flour. When you cannot separate the parts of a substance easily, you are less sure it is a mixture and not a compound. Salt dissolved in water looks like water. Taste identifies it as salt water. Heating the water until it has all disappeared as steam leaves a **residue** of salt that is a more reliable test.

A mixture has been formed when two or more elements or compounds are mixed together but no chemical change has taken place. The mixed elements or compounds do not lose their individual characteristics and can be separated by a physical means.

Do this investigation.

These supplies are needed:

- bottle containing a material prepared by the teacher
- toothpicks

Follow these instructions and answer the questions. Put a check in the box when each step is completed.

☐ 1. Choose a partner to work with. Obtain a bottle of material from your teacher.

☐ 2. Using a toothpick, separate the material in the bottle if you can.

1.49 Is this a compound, element, or mixture? _____ .

1.50 What was the physical means by which the contents were separated?

_____

_____

1.51 What were the four items in the bottle? a. _____ , b. _____ ,

c. _____ , and d. _____ .

1.52 Without using toothpicks, what other methods could you have used to separate this substance?

_____

_____

_____

_____

_____

TEACHER CHECK _____ _____

initials   date

Mixtures Experiment

MATTER IN CHANGE

Natural factors and humankind cause matter to change. Your body is growing and changing constantly. Sometimes you like what is happening and sometimes you do not. Weather conditions change from sunshine to rain and may bring floods that cause misery for many people. Humans can do nothing about weather conditions, but they may be able either to prevent or to relieve some of the results. A dam built in the right place may prevent disaster. The physical, chemical, and nuclear changes of matter are frequently not controllable by human beings. God rules the world and He manages all change. The wonder of all creation is that God created humans to be the caretakers of the energy and power found in nature. The responsibility is great, and we are all accountable to God for what we do with it. Our bodies and our lives are part of our responsibility. What we do with our lives is most important. Careful thought regarding a vocation should begin with asking God for guidance that we may become good caretakers of our lives and use God's wonders for His glory.

Physical change. The changes most easily recognized are physical changes. A change in size, shape, color, or form does not change the chemical composition of matter, only the physical properties which are often obvious. Physical change is also more easily accomplished than chemical change. Heat applied to matter usually causes it to expand (except water, which expands as it freezes). When matter expands, it takes up more space. As heat is applied the molecules move faster, and bounce against each other harder, and the space between the molecules increases. Cooling will slow this process and will return the matter to its original form. No chemical change has taken place. The matter has not changed composition, just form.

Matter has many physical characteristics. *Soluble* substances can dissolve in liquids. The molecules separate from each other and scatter among the liquid molecules. If a substance cannot dissolve, it is said to be *insoluble.*

Matter changes from one form to another. More heat changes a liquid to a gas. Changing from one form to another is called a *phase.* The change is made by heat. For every substance, the amount of heat added or removed to make the change happen is different. Heat capacity is the amount needed for change by each substance and is also called *specific heat.* Specific heats are recorded in tables for easy referral so that the scientist can conduct their experiment with accuracy.

The pressure cooker is a good example of matter in change. Water boils at 100° Celsius at sea level in an open container. Under such conditions, however fast it boils, the temperature stays the same. Water can be made hotter than 100°C or boiling. A pressure cooker works on this principle. In the closed container, the water boils and changes to steam. As heat continues to be supplied, the temperature goes up to be approximately 107°C. The food cooks more quickly. If steam builds up too much pressure, the safety valve will blow out, preventing damage.

Do this investigation.

These supplies are needed:

- ■ pressure cooker or instant pot

Follow these directions and answer the questions. Put a check in the box when each step is completed.

☐ 1. Examine a pressure cooker at home or in a store.

☐ 2. Ask an adult or your teacher to explain the principles of operation or refer to the pamphlet that came with it from the manufacturer.

1.53 Why does the cooker have a valve with a gauge on it?

_____

_____

1.54 What is the purpose of the rubber gasket on the lid?

_____

1.55 What kind of changes occur in a pressure cooker?

_____

_____

_____

1.56 Read the high altitude directions for baking a cake mix. Why are they different from regular directions?

_____

_____

_____

Physical Changes Experiment

Do this investigation.

These supplies are needed:

- jar
- iron filings

Follow the directions and do the activity. Put a check in the box when each step is completed.

☐ 1. Prepare your Science Record form so you can record your entries.

☐ 2. Rinse the jar or glass with water and shake out as much moisture as you can without drying it entirely. Caution: Do not hit the sink or any hard surface that could cause the jar to break in your hand.

☐ 3. Sprinkle some iron filings into the jar carefully so that they will stick to the side of the jar in the moisture. Set aside and observe daily until you see the iron filings turn reddish-brown.

☐ 4. Write your result on the SR form.

1.57 Four iron atoms joined the three oxygen molecules to form two molecules of iron oxide (Fe_2O_3) or rust. For your conclusion write this change in a chemical equation.

_____

TEACHER CHECK _____ _____
initials   date

Chemical Changes Experiment

Chemical change. Chemical change takes place when the *appearance* and *composition* of matter change. New substances are formed but atoms are neither made nor lost. Some form of energy is released to bring about a chemical change. Electrolysis is a good example. The chemical equation for this process is

$$H_2O \rightarrow 2H + O.$$

Read it this way: water (H_2O) splits into ($\rightarrow$) two atoms of hydrogen (2H) and one atom of oxygen (O). The short form is called a *chemical equation*.

Consider this situation: A silver spoon is left in a dish of custard. Custard contains eggs and eggs contain sulfur. The spoon turns black (tarnishes). Read this equation of what happened:

$2 Ag + S \rightarrow Ag_2S$. If you said two atoms of silver plus one atom of sulfur forms ($\rightarrow$) silver sulfide, you were correct.

Chemical equations represent the chemical changes that take place constantly. Rusting and tarnishing are two examples. Fermentation (which aids in making yeast breads), digestion, souring of milk, spoiling of food, photosynthesis, and the manufacture of many items, such as glass and plastics, are additional examples.

Water can be changed physically from solid to liquid to gas but the molecule is not changed. The water molecule is split by electrolysis into its atoms, hydrogen and oxygen, in a chemical change. Recently the nucleus of an atom was split into two fragments of approximately equal mass. The splitting of the atom produced energy. Although this feat was accomplished in the 1940s, we refer to it as *recent* compared to the more than two thousand years since Aristotle made important contributions to the entire scheme of science study. *Nuclear fission* is the name of this process, considered the third way matter changes. This principle is the basis for the atomic bomb.

Acid and bases. Acids are very important to the chemist. Acids are very common and very useful. Sometimes they seem destructive because strong acids are quite active. They taste sour. Vinegar is acetic acid (CH_3COOH). Vinegar is used for its tart (sour) flavor in many foods, especially pickles. It also serves as a preservative. Hydrochloric acid made in your stomach aids digestion. Sulfuric acid is used as a dehydrating agent in storage batteries. Sulfuric acid can burn your clothes or your skin if splattered. All acids should be handled with care. Chemical formulas for acids, such as HCl (hydrochloric), H_2SO_4 (sulfuric), and CH_3COOH (acetic) all have one atom in common. What is it? If you said *hydrogen,* you are correct.

Tests are made to determine whether solutions are acidic by using litmus paper or a liquid called phenolphthalein. Acid tests are very common in the laboratory where either one may be used easily. Acid tests are also used in the home, in industry, and for medical diagnosis. Litmus is sold at the drug store and even made up in kits so a person may make regular acid tests under the supervision of the doctor. Blue litmus turns red when the solution is acid. Blue litmus does not change color if the solution is

a base. Red litmus paper turns blue for a base but does not change for an acid.

The pH scale shown in Science LIFEPAC 803, shows how acids and bases are evaluated for strength in terms of the hydronium (H_3O) concentration. Acids and bases are on opposite ends of the scale. A base is a substance that tastes bitter and feels slippery like oil. All bases contain at least one metal plus hydrogen and oxygen combined as a hydroxide ion (OH). If we have two hydroxide ions, the OH is placed in parentheses (OH) and the 2 becomes a subscript of the OH ion $(OH)_2$.

Warning: The sour taste for acid and the bitter taste for the base have been given as characteristics of the two substances. Although this fact is true, it is not presented to tell you to test unknown substances by tasting. Do *not* taste any *unknown* substance at any time.

The midpoint of the pH scale is neutral. When acids and bases are combined, the properties of each are destroyed. The chemical compound formed is a salt, and the salt has its own characteristics. Sodium chloride (table salt) is the one known best, but it is only one of many. Salt is used to season food to improve its flavor; but if salt touches an open sore, it will hurt. Bushes and grass die if the salt used to melt snow and ice on sidewalks and streets get on the plants. Acids and bases are helpful but must be handled with respect because they can be equally harmful.

Complete these statements.

1.58 Every acid has an atom of a. _____ ; every base has a

b. _____ and c. _____ ion.

1.59 An acid combined with a base forms a(n) _____ .

Write the letter of the correct choice on the line.

1.60 _____ NaOH   a. acid

1.61 _____ HCl   b. base

1.62 _____ $Ca(OH)_2$ c. salt

1.63 _____ H_2SO_4

1.64 _____ NaCl

1.65 _____ $CuSO_4$

1.66 _____ CH_3COOH

1.67 _____ $Al(OH)_2$

Review the material in this section in preparation for the Self Test. The Self Test will check your mastery of this particular section. The items missed on this Self Test will indicate specific areas where restudy is needed for mastery.

SELF TEST 1

Match these items (each answer, 2 points).

1.01	_____ nucleus and electrons in orbit	a. adaptability
1.02	_____ maximum speed limit	b. liter
1.03	_____ positive personal skill	c. Aristotle
1.04	_____ turns blue litmus red	d. technology
1.05	_____ scientific measurement	e. resiliency
1.06	_____ quart plus	f. 110 km/h
1.07	_____ first to use an orderly system of study	g. atom
1.08	_____ turns red litmus blue	h. cubic centimeter
1.09	_____ bounce back with good humor	I. acid
1.010	_____ applied science	j. base
		k. 88 km/h

Write true or false (each answer, 1 point).

1.011 _____ The word _atom_ means to _fuse_.

1.012 _____ An acid and base combine to form a salt.

1.013 _____ The midpoint of the pH scale is neutral.

1.014 _____ Baking a cake is the same at low or high altitude.

1.015 _____ The smallest particle of matter is the atom.

1.016 _____ God controls the bonds that hold a molecule together.

1.017 _____ Sugar water is a mixture.

Complete these sentences (each answer, 3 points).

1.018 Science is the systematized knowledge derived from a. _____ ,
b. _____ , and c. _____ .

1.019 The main units in the metric system are length a. _____ , volume b. _____ ,
and mass c. _____ .

1.020 During the process of electrolysis of water, a. _____ and
b. _____ are collected.

1.021 Matter changes in a. _____ , b. _____ , and
c. _____ ways.

1.022 The Nobel Prize was won by a. _____ for finding that electrons
in atoms stay in b. _____ .

1.023 The process by which an atom splits to produce energy is known as _____
_____ .

1.024 Scientists estimate that _____ compounds are known.

1.025 The upward force that make a cork float is called _____ .

1.026 The expression $2Ag + S \rightarrow Ag_2S$ is called a(n) _____ .

1.027 The symbol for water (H_2O) is called a(n) _____ .

Answer these questions (each answer, 5 points).

1.028 Why is the metric system a preferred form of measurement?

_____

_____

1.029 What are five properties of matter?

_____

1.030 How does a pressure cooker cook food faster?

_____

_____

77/96 **SCORE** _____ **TEACHER** _____ _____
initials   date

2. PHYSICAL SCIENCE

Sciences that deal with **inanimate** matter or energy are classified as *physical science*. The forces of nature are a mystery to us as we watch a storm develop and later see the results. Automobiles are useful vehicles that most of us depend on for transportation. However, when motors stop running in a deserted area with no help in sight, automobiles are a mystery to us. Our goal in this section is to remove some of the mystery by reviewing what we know about matter and energy and becoming more skilled in using the forces of physical science.

Vocations involving machines and electricity are numerous. Engineers of all kinds are in demand. Auto mechanics are needed. The newspaper advertises continually for workers in the computer field.

Employment is available in industry and will be for a long time. The job level you strive for and attain will be determined by your effort. *You* are the force that moves through the distance to accomplish work. Energy stored within you is *potential*. Change it to *kinetic* energy so that it will accomplish good.

King Josiah was only eight years old when he began his thirty-one year reign in Jerusalem. He was a faithful servant of God and did what was right in God's sight. The people had deserted God, and the kings before Josiah were evil. The Temple had been neglected and was in need of repairs. Second Chronicles chapter 34 describes how the people worked. Workmen repaired and mended; overseers supervised; laborers were bearers of burdens; and scribes, officers, and porters helped. Read 2 Chronicles 34:1–13. The first part of verse 12 says, "And the men did the work faithfully...." No job is too big or too small if it is done *faithfully*.

SECTION OBJECTIVES

Review these objectives. When you have completed this section, you should be able to:

5. List examples of potential and kinetic energy and show work accomplished.
6. Explain the forms of conversion of energy.
7. Describe magnetism and its relation to electricity.
8. List vocations available in science and technology dependent on electricity.
9. Explain the meaning of work scientifically and in view of Christian responsibility.
10. List simple machines and explain each in terms of examples from daily life.

VOCABULARY

Study these words to enhance your learning success in this section.

adhesion (ad hē' zhun). A sticking together; molecular attraction exerted between surfaces of bodies in contact.

alloy (al' oi). A metal made by melting together two or more metals, or a metal and some other substance.

depict (di pikt'). To represent by drawing, painting, or describing; show; picture; portray.

disrupt (dis rupt'). To break up; split.

environmentalist (en vī' run men' tu list). An advocate of environmentalism (a view that the environment, rather than hereditary factors or individual initiative, is the dominating force in effecting change).

fission (fish' un). A splitting apart; division into its parts; the splitting that occurs when the nucleus of an atom under bombardment absorbs a neutron and divides into two nearly equal parts.

generalization (jen' ur lu zā' shun). The act or process of generalizing; a general idea, statement, principle, rule.

inanimate (in an' u mit). Not alive or animate.

lubricant (lü' bru kunt). Oil, grease, and so forth for putting on parts of machines to make them slippery so they will work easily.

materialistic (mu tir' ē lis' tik). The tendency to care too much for the things of this world and neglect spiritual needs.

phenomenon (fu nom' u non). A fact, event, or circumstance that can be observed.

retract (ri trakt'). To withdraw; to take back; to draw back.

verified (ver' u fīd). To prove to be true; confirm.

FORMS OF ENERGY

The physical world around us is composed of matter and energy. In Section I, you have studied the characteristics of matter and hinted about energy. Energy is defined as the *ability to do work*.

The Grand Canyon in northwest Arizona is a wonder of the work of nature. The Colorado River travels this mammoth canyon. Upstream (north) on the same river is the Glen Canyon Dam, and downstream (southwest) is the Hoover Dam (see Figure 4).

Potential energy. Water has piled up behind Glen Canyon Dam in Arizona to form Lake Powell. The canyons of this area are filled to a depth of more than 1,500 feet in some places. This trapped water exerts tremendous pressure on the dam. Hoover Dam in southeastern Nevada holds back the water to form another very large deep lake, Lake Mead. Both lakes are used to provide irrigation for desert crops. They are also used as recreation areas for camping, fishing, boating, and swimming. Recreation and irrigation are not the primary reasons for construction of the dams. The dams are located in desolate areas where electricity was not easily available. At the base of the dams are very large turbines and dynamos that produce electric power for the region and other states a distance away.

Kinetic energy. The energy water possesses because of its movement is kinetic energy. At some time in history, a large flow of water carved through the area of the Grand Canyon through which the Colorado River now flows. Unless you have seen the Grand Canyon, you cannot imagine the amount of work that has been accomplished by the river. The gorge is over 200 miles long and one mile deep.

Energy can be changed from one form to another. The water in Lake Mead and Lake Powell is at rest. The water possesses potential energy because of its position behind the dam.

Water released against the turbines supplies force to produce electrical energy by mechanical means. *Potential* energy is changed to *kinetic* energy.

Kinetic energy is energy in motion. Since matter is composed of molecules, we know that to produce energy we must make molecules move. In the late 1700's, Count Rutherford of Bavaria, Germany noticed that large quantities of heat were produced when a hole was bored in iron to make a cannon. He did not agree with earlier scientists who said that heat was a fluid that flowed into the object as it became warmer. The Count made the suggestion that heat was produced by motion within the object itself. Further experimentation found Count Rutherford to be correct. Heat was an energy itself produced by another energy. Heat is the energy of moving molecules. Different forms of energy produce heat.

 Complete this activity.

2.1 This map shows the Colorado River from the Hoover Dam to Lake Powell. Write in the blanks whether the state of the water of the river is potential or kinetic energy. The letters on the map correspond to the letters of the blanks.

a. _____   b. _____

c. _____   d. _____

e. _____   f. _____

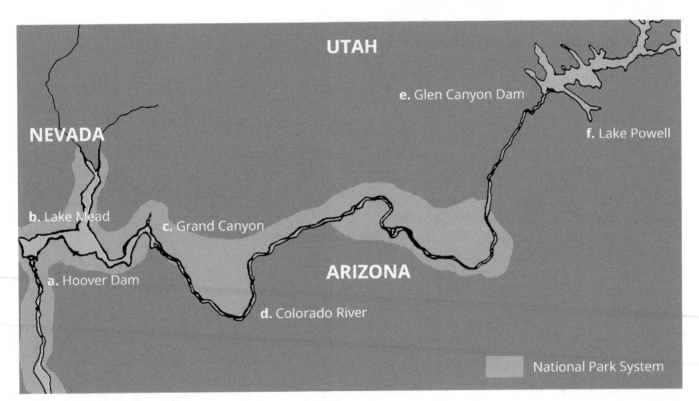

Figure 4 | Colorado River

Mechanical energy. Energy produced by mechanical means is classified as *mechanical* energy. Moving water directed against the blades of a turbine makes the dynamo turn to generate electricity and is mechanical energy. Mechanical energy is converted to electricity. Bicycles are sometimes equipped with small generators that produce enough electricity to turn on the light. The electricity is not generated if you do not turn the pedals.

When mechanical energy is discharged, heat is produced through friction. Friction is caused by rubbing substances together. Molecules are set in rapid motion and produce heat. The faster the molecules move, the hotter the substance becomes.

Heat energy. We determined in Section I that space exists between molecules and that molecules are in constant motion. Imagine the molecules bouncing back and forth in this space. The faster they move, the greater the amount of impact. Toss a hard ball to your friend gently, and they will catch it without feeling much impact. Throw the ball with speed, and hands will sting because the impact was greater. A rubber ball thrown at a wall bounces back to you at about the same rate that you throw it. Throw it at the wall with speed and the ball will bounce back a greater distance than a slow ball. Think of the balls as molecules. Within a limited space, they are moving moderately until some form of energy makes them move faster. The substance becomes hotter.

Carrying the molecular theory of heat further, we begin to see what *cold* is. What happens when the molecules slow down? We have less heat, lower temperature, and some degree of cold. *Absolute zero* (-273°C) is the lowest point of cold matter can reach. Scientists have come within one-millionth of a degree of absolute zero. Since one characteristic of matter is that molecules are in constant motion, would you like to speculate as to what would happen if all motion were stopped with the molecule?

Would it disintegrate? Maybe you will be the research scientist to answer that question some day.

An interesting effect of heat energy is the ability to be transferred through the three forms of matter.

Complete this investigation.

These supplies are needed:

- ring stand
- glass beaker

- heat screen or wire gauze with ceramic center
- heat source (alcohol lamp burner, wickless)

- thermometer
- dropper (pipet)

Follow these directions. Put a check in the box when each step is completed. Use the Science Record form to write your experiment.

☐ 1. The problem is to find if heat can be transferred through solids, liquids, and gases. Set up the ring stand with the metal screen on the ring to hold the beaker. A fireproof glass may be used in place of the beaker.

☐ 2. Fill the beaker halfway and place a thermometer in the water. If your heat source is a candle, it will take a long time to heat the water. You may not see it boil. A Bunsen burner is best: however, an electric hotplate can be used. We will assume the Bunsen burner, screen, ring stand, and beaker are being used.

☐ 3. Apply heat. The metal screen will get hot. To test this fact place a drop of water on the screen. What happens?

☐ 4. Bring the water to a boil. What temperature do you have? Can you see the steam?

☐ 5. Carefully pass your hand over the air immediately above the beaker. Does the air feel hot? Is it steam?

☐ 6. Conclusion: Explain what happens from the time the heat is applied under the wire screen, the beaker, and the water, and is felt above all these substances.

☐ 7. Ask your teacher to check your Science Record form for completeness of data and accuracy of your conclusion.

TEACHER CHECK _____ _____
                    initials   date

Heat Transfer Experiment

The preceding investigation shows that heat can be transferred through the three forms of matter: solid, liquid, and gas. Another important factor to remember is that almost all substances expand when heated and contract when cooled. Water is one of the exceptions. Water *expands* as it *cools* to freezing. The most common substance on earth is an exception to a basic consistent rule. Scientists have an explanation based on the molecular theory. As the temperature of water approaches freezing, from 4°C to 0°C, water expands. Ice forms with a lower density than water and floats on top of the water. Have you ever noticed a thin layer of ice on a puddle when temperatures dropped to freezing overnight? The ice freezes on top and becomes an insulator for the water below, which cools more slowly. Lakes and ponds do not freeze to the bottom. Rivers have been seen continuing their journey under a thick layer of ice. Since the water under the ice remains liquid, living things do not freeze to death. Scientists who can explain a **phenomenon** such as this with the molecular theory are confirming the greatness of God in the orderly creation of the universe. If He has made this provision in nature so that aquatic life can survive, how much more has He provided for us? Memorize Luke 12:7.

Heat is transferred from one object to another by three methods: *conduction, convection,* and *radiation.* The last investigation was an example of *conduction.* Heat was transferred through the three forms of matter.

Convection occurs when gases or liquids are heated, become less dense and lighter than the cooler gas or liquid adjacent to them, and rise. This movement establishes a circular motion known as a convection current. A sudden change in temperature outdoors causes convection currents or winds. The greater the sudden drop of temperature, the stronger the winds. This principle is also the basis for hot air heating systems used in many buildings. Hot air also fills large balloons by convection currents from small furnaces. Ballooning has become a very popular sport.

Radiation is heat traveling in waves through the air. Heat travels at the speed of light, 186,000 miles per second. Radiation is the most important method of transference because this method is the way the Earth is warmed by the Sun. Without the Sun's warmth no life would exist. Other forms of energy produce heat. Heat energy is so basic to the other energy forms that more time is spent studying about it.

Complete these sentences.

2.2 Heat is transferred from pot to water by _____ .

2.3 Heat is transferred by _____ when it causes winds.

2.4 Heat reaches the earth from the sun by a. _____ and travels at the speed of b. _____ .

2.5 Most substances a. _____ when heated and b. _____ when cooled.

2.6 The exception to this rule is _____ .

Write this verse.

2.7   You have memorized Luke 12:7. Write it in the space provided.

_____

_____

_____

TEACHER CHECK _____ _____
                              initials   date

Chemical energy. Early scientists who had concluded that the atom was the smallest particle of matter made a law after much experimentation. The law was that _matter can neither be created nor destroyed_. Sir Ernest Rutherford in 1911 was the first to construct a model of the atom **depicting** a nucleus surrounded by electrons whirling around in orbits. Now smaller particles are known to compose the atom. When atomic **fission** was finally achieved, scientists believed that the law of conservation had to be changed. Part of the mass of the atom changed to energy. The process is called a nuclear or atomic reaction. Atomic fission was the first time the mass changed after a reaction. The law then was changed to state that _neither matter nor energy can be either created or destroyed, but they can be changed from one to another_. Chemical equations represent what has happened when substances are combined and react to form other substances. The orderliness of science is again very evident. Since matter is not destroyed, both sides of a chemical equation will balance. The same number of atoms of each element must appear on each side. The process may go through several steps but the left side of the equation shows what is combined, and the right shows the final result, or product.

Numbers appear in two positions in the chemical equation. Either they are in front of the symbol to indicate the number of molecules or atoms, or they are written as a subscript to denote the number of atoms in the molecule involved. Oxygen is found in air as a gas and is part of many chemical reactions. A single free atom of oxygen does not occur naturally. Two atoms (O_2) make up the oxygen molecule. The rusting of iron filings which you witnessed in an earlier experiment is an example. The equation is $4Fe + 3O_2 \rightarrow 2\ Fe_2O_3$. The equation is balanced. Changing the symbols to words it would read: 4 atoms of iron plus 3 molecules of oxygen yield 2 molecules of iron oxide. To find the number of atoms in the molecule, multiply the number of molecules by the subscript for each element. In iron oxide 4 atoms of iron plus 6 (3×2) atoms of oxygen yield 4 (2×2) atoms of iron + 6 (3×2) atoms of oxygen, or 2 molecules of iron oxide.

Complete the chemical statements by writing the correct numbers in the blanks.

2.8 $C + O_2 \rightarrow CO_2$

a. _____ atom(s) of carbon plus b. _____ atom(s) of oxygen yield c. _____ molecule(s) of carbon dioxide.

2.9 $2H_2 + O_2 \rightarrow 2H_2O$

a. _____ molecule(s) *or* b. _____ atom(s) of hydrogen plus c. _____ molecule(s) of oxygen yield d. _____ molecule(s) of water.

2.10   The numbers in the next chemical equation are larger but the equation is balanced the same way.

Bread rises because yeast acts on the sugar to produce carbon dioxide and alcohol.

Complete the statement.
$C_6H_{12}O_6 \rightarrow 2C_2H_6O + 2\ CO_2$
sugar → alcohol + carbon dioxide

a. _____ molecule(s) of dextrose sugar yields b. _____ molecule(s) of ethyl alcohol plus

c. _____ molecule(s) of carbon dioxide through the action of yeast. The small amount of alcohol evaporates during baking.

Atomic energy. Nuclear fission has been discussed in your Science LIFEPACs several times. The structure of the atom has been presented in a number of different ways. Do not continue reading until you are certain that you recall what has been taught about atomic structure and energy change. Review Science LIFEPACs 801, 802, 803, and 805 if necessary. When you feel comfortable about your knowledge of this subject matter, you may proceed.

Scientists are very wary of making **generalizations** without actual proof. An unproved general statement maybe proved wrong and the scientist will have to **retract** their statement. If a scientist retracts statements too often, their reputation will be smeared. Some basic generalizations have been made because the occurrence of the phenomenon has been frequent.

The generalized statement that *large events have their origin in the reaction of tiny particles* is again **verified** by the release of atomic energy.

When the atomic bomb (uranium bomb) was produced, it represented the first practical use of the release of atomic energy. The first bomb was dropped on Hiroshima, Japan, on August 6, 1945. One atomic bomb is equal in striking power to 2,000 of the largest TNT bombs known in 1945. The bomb dropped on Hiroshima killed 60,000 people outright, injured 100,000 more, and left 200,000 homeless. A few days later, a second atomic bomb was dropped on the city of Nagasaki in Japan. The Japanese government surrendered, and World War II was ended. After this time a hydrogen bomb was developed many times more powerful than the uranium bomb (atomic bomb).

Atomic energy is the energy tied up in an inactive state in the nucleus of the atom. Energy holds the parts of the atoms together. The nucleus of the atom contains very little energy, but great amounts of energy are released when a chain reaction occurs. In a chain reaction one split atom splits the next atom and on and on.

When the atom splits, we call it *fission* from the Latin *fissio,* to *cleave.* The release of energy rays, or radiation, is very dangerous to living organisms and must be carefully controlled; or it will have destructive effects on the population and other living things.

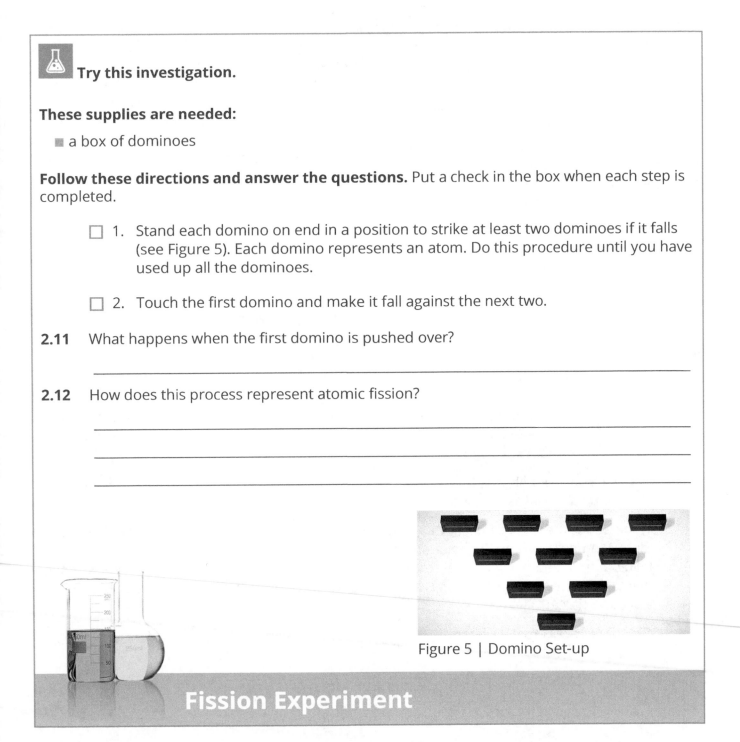

Try this investigation.

These supplies are needed:

- ■ a box of dominoes

Follow these directions and answer the questions. Put a check in the box when each step is completed.

☐ 1. Stand each domino on end in a position to strike at least two dominoes if it falls (see Figure 5). Each domino represents an atom. Do this procedure until you have used up all the dominoes.

☐ 2. Touch the first domino and make it fall against the next two.

2.11 What happens when the first domino is pushed over?

_____

2.12 How does this process represent atomic fission?

_____

_____

_____

Figure 5 | Domino Set-up

Fission Experiment

Uses of atomic energy. The commercial development of radioactive elements has been helpful to medical research. Doctors can trace them through the body to diagnose disease and sometimes use them to treat cancer, skin diseases, and glandular illnesses. They are now also used in industry and in energy production.

In spite of the peaceful use of atomic energy, great controversy exists about it. Protest groups are attempting to stop the construction of nuclear power plants. Why?

A strong nation with great power has responsibility. We cannot use our power carelessly as individuals or as a nation. Cain killed his brother Abel, and when God asked Cain where his brother was he said in Genesis 4:9, "...I know not: Am I my brother's keeper?"

God then cursed Cain. We are expected to care about what happens to our fellow man. The use of the atomic bomb or the hydrogen bomb and the benefits of nuclear energy are questioned by many people. The controversy is great enough to catch the attention of our lawmakers. What do you think about it?

The release of energy from the atom has been a great achievement for science. We have discussed the harmful effects of the atomic bomb, but we should not ignore the very valuable peacetime uses of atomic energy. Remember the great things that the scientists accomplished in making this energy available to the world. To God we give the glory for the miracles of creation and the mysteries of the tiny atom.

 Complete this activity.

2.13 Write a report of 500 words or more stating your thoughts about these questions. Make an outline first in an orderly manner. Write your paper following the outline. Your last paragraph should state your conclusion.

Use books at your library, the *World Book Encyclopedia,* or online sources to read about Hiroshima and Nagasaki and the research about the results that followed.

Think about these questions: What happened to the people who survived? What were President Truman's reasons for releasing the A-bomb? What are the arguments for and against using atomic energy? Why are protest groups trying to stop the building of nuclear energy plants? What is the Christian view concerning our responsibility to other people? What is your view as a citizen?

Give your report to your teacher.

TEACHER CHECK _____ _____
                                            initials   date

Entropy. The nuclear bombs are the extreme examples of energy conversion. The energy released is not all usable. Much heat energy is made unavailable. The use of the bomb for destruction contributes to increased entropy or disorder in the universe.

A discussion of entropy mystifies the scientists who do not believe in God. They do not understand the orderliness of the universe. They see disorder as a cycle that will continue uncontrolled and will lead eventually to total destruction. They do not recognize the power of God to stop destruction if it is His will.

A German scientist is quoted as saying, "A little science leads away from God: more science leads back to Him." The more we study science, the more we must acknowledge that only God in heaven could have made anything as intricate, consistent, and well-organized as this universe.

 Complete these statements.

2.14 Nuclear bombs are extreme examples of _____ conversion.

2.15 Doctors can diagnose disease by tracing _____ elements through the body.

2.16 Another name for the disorder in the universe is _____ .

2.17 The more we study science the more we learn about _____ .

MAGNETS AND ELECTRICITY

Magnets and electricity have been studied for centuries as separate isolated forces. As time went by their common factors were observed. Scientists found magnetism and electricity could produce each other. Study these comparisons.

1. Like poles repel each other.
2. Unlike poles attract each other.
3. A magnet has a field of force.
4. A magnet moved near a coil of wire causes electric current to flow in the wire

Magnetism

1. Similar electric charges repel.
2. Unlike electric charges attract.
3. A wire carrying an electric current has a magnetic field around it.
4. A coil of wire carrying a current and wound around an iron core will make the coil magnetic.

Electricity

Behavior of magnets. Lodestone is the name given to rocks that have natural magnetism. They are identified by testing with bits of iron that will cling to the magnetic rock. Lodestones also have a north and south pole. These magnetic rocks are difficult to find because they resemble other rocks. The magnets commonly used in games, in children's toys, or for classroom use are artificially made and are shaped as bars or horseshoes. Since magnets can be useful for many purposes, a practical material for mass producing them had to be found. The alloy of iron, aluminum, nickel, copper, and cobalt is called *Alnico.* This alloy is made into magnets commercially.

The way a magnet behaves has determined its usefulness. In Science LIFEPAC 806, the magnetic field was traced by using iron filings. The lines of force repelled each other between similar poles and passed from one pole to the other when poles were opposite. A magnet suspended in air by a piece of string takes a north-south position in line with the earth's magnetic poles.

Magnetic theory. The explanation given for magnetism is a theory. Several theories have been suggested, but the one that has proved most reliable after a great deal of investigation is that each atom is a tiny magnet. Among the evidence that points to this theory is the *domain* theory you have studied. In an demagnetized bar of iron, the atoms are facing different ways of disorder. In a magnetized bar of iron, the atoms are lined up. A needle stroked in one direction with a magnet will become a magnet because the atoms in the needle have been pulled into line.

A magnet can be demagnetized by hammering on it or dropping it several times. This change would indicate that the atoms can be put out of alignment. Heating a magnet also removes the magnetism. The heat causes the molecules to move about rapidly and takes them out of position.

Magnets that are used to hold papers on the refrigerator door demonstrate another principle of behavior. Magnetism penetrates certain materials, such as glass, wood, paper, air, and water. If a sheet of iron is placed between the magnet and the tacks you are trying to pick up, the tacks will fall off. The magnetism does not pass through material that has been magnetized. The iron sheet keeps some of the magnetism.

Try this investigation.

These supplies are needed:

- bar magnet
- paper
- wood
- iron filings
- other demagnetized materials

Follow these directions and complete the activities. Put a check in the box when each step is completed.

☐ 1. This investigation is a review. Place a magnet between two books of equal thickness. Lay a sheet of paper on the books over the magnet (see Figure 6). Have the books as far apart as possible but still supporting the paper adequately.

sheet of paper

magnet

Figure 6 | Experiment Layout

☐ 2. Sprinkle iron filings on the surface of the paper and tap to produce the field of force.

☐ 3. Prepare your Science Record form and begin to record your experiment. The problem is: what materials allow magnetism to penetrate?

☐ 4. Use the same procedure as in Step 1 but substitute other materials for the paper. You may do it directly such as on the wood desk top. Hold the magnet underneath the desk top and sprinkle a few iron filings on top of the desk.

☐ 5. Test at least five different substances.

☐ 6. Conclusion must be a statement answering the problem.

☐ 7. Complete the Science Record.

TEACHER CHECK _____ _____

initials   date

Magnetism Experiment

Electromagnets. *Induced magnetism* is another property. A needle stroked by a magnet becomes magnetized. A coil of wire wound around an iron nail will change the nail into an electromagnet while the current is flowing. When the current is turned off, the nail is no longer a magnet. Tools can unexpectedly become magnets. Screwdrivers may be purchased as magnets. The screw is held in place by the magnetized screwdriver when you are working in hard-to-reach places. A screwdriver may become magnetized while working with electrical equipment. Why?

Electromagnets have practical value. First, the strength of the magnet can be changed, since the electromagnets can be manufactured. When the current is stronger, or the coil of wire is longer, or both, the magnet will be stronger.

Second, magnetism can be turned on or off. Very heavy loads, such as scrap iron, are loaded into furnaces at steel mills with large electromagnets. A flip of the switch turns off the current, and the scrap iron drops. The flexibility of the electromagnet as a temporary magnet made it ideal for the telegraph, telephone, and electric motor.

Third, the poles of an electromagnet can be reversed. This quality made possible the development of the electric motor. Permanent magnets have a definite north and south pole. The poles do not change. The electromagnet has poles also, but their location depends on the direction the current is flowing in the coil. By reversing the current, the position of poles is reversed. This principle is used in switching the poles of the two magnets in the motor to keep the armature turning.

 Complete these activities.

2.18 List the three advantages of the electromagnet.

a. _____

b. _____

c. _____

2.19 List two ways permanent magnets are used.

a. _____

b. _____

2.20 List three ways electromagnets are used in industry.

a. _____

b. _____

c. _____

SCIENCE 810

LIFEPAC TEST

NAME _____

DATE _____

SCORE _____

SCIENCE 810: LIFEPAC TEST

Match these items (each answer, 2 points).

1. _____ heat transfer
2. _____ current
3. _____ check out scientific facts
4. _____ mass divided by volume
5. _____ an account of an investigation
6. _____ water pushes up against mass
7. _____ ability to do work
8. _____ 55 mph
9. _____ like poles
10. _____ found in molecules

a. Science Record
b. energy
c. buoyancy
d. electrons in orbit
e. convection
f. density
g. repel
h. verify
i. flow of electricity
j. attract
k. 88 km/h

Write true or false (each answer, 1 point).

11. _____ Technology and health services are growing areas of opportunity for jobs.
12. _____ A Christian has an obligation to work faithfully.
13. _____ The universe is filled with disorder leading to destruction.
14. _____ Tests given in school have little relation to choosing a job.
15. _____ Health services have many job opportunities.
16. _____ God created the universe with the purpose of having it destroyed.
17. _____ A résumé tells about you.
18. _____ Nothing you can do now will prepare you for a career.
19. _____ Good work should be rewarded.
20. _____ The carbon-oxygen cycle is an example of destruction in nature.

Match the letter to the item. The letter may be used more than once (each answer, 2 points).

21.	_____ water behind the dam	a. potential energy
22.	_____ river eroding rock	b. kinetic energy
23.	_____ student sleeping	
24.	_____ loose rock on mountainside	
25.	_____ water released against turbine	

- -

26.	_____ solid state to liquid state	a. physical change
27.	_____ splitting the atom	b. chemical change
28.	_____ photosynthesis	c. nuclear change
29.	_____ burning	
30.	_____ liquid state to gas state	

- -

31.	_____ egg beater	a. lever
32.	_____ ramp	b. wheel and axle
33.	_____ ax head	c. inclined plane
34.	_____ nutcracker	d. screw
35.	_____ winch	e. wedge
36.	_____ wheel barrow	f. pulley
37.	_____ doorknob	g. gear

Complete these statements (each answer, 3 points).

38. Proficiency in science skills must be added to the two personal skills of

    a. _____ and b. _____ .

39. The scientific method includes three skills:

    a. _____ ,

    b. _____ , and c. _____ .

40. The basic metric measure for length is a. _____ , for mass is

    b. _____ , and for volume is c. _____ .

41. The job market is _____ for young adults and recent college graduates.

42. The atom's nucleus contains a. _____ and b. _____ .

43. Water can be broken up into a. _____ and b. _____ by

    c. _____ .

44. An extreme example of energy conversion is the _____ .

45. Physical energy produces _____ when hands are rubbed together.

Static electricity. The term *static electricity* is another example of the conclusions early scientists reached before the nature of the atom was learned. *Static* means to *remain stationary*—in one place. Static electricity is always present, but you do not notice it until it jumps from one object to another, it moves across space to the opposite charge. The spark can be seen in a dark room, and you are aware it is a form of electricity. If it moves from one place to another, it can hardly be standing still! The scientist is really contrasting static electricity with current electricity, which flows through a wire. Possibly the word *static* is not entirely accurate, but it is widely accepted.

Atoms are made of negatively charged electrons and positively charged protons, which occur in equal numbers in an atom. The electrons whirl around the protons and other particles held within the nucleus of the atom. Electrons are easily removed from their orbits, but protons cannot be moved without also moving the atom.

One behavior of electrons and protons is basic to understanding electricity. Similar charges of electricity repel each other, and unlike charges attract. If you rub your shoes on the carpeting, especially when the atmosphere is dry and electrons are more easily moved, you will pick up electrons that will collect on your skin. Touch a doorknob, another person, or a lamp switch and you are discharged. This effect can be annoying. Antistatic substances have been developed that remove the surplus electrons. Many products on the market today are applied to carpeting or are used in the rinse cycle of the washing machine to prevent static build-up.

Lightning. Lightning is a form of static electricity that occurs during certain weather conditions. The thunderstorm clouds become positively charged in the upper areas and negatively charged below. The cloud moves across the land and *repels* the negative charges near the ground but *attracts* the positive charges that come to the surface. A string of negative charges leaves the cloud suddenly and leaps close to the ground. This lightning that does not touch ground is called a *leader*. When the leader approaches the ground, the positive charges jump the gap to the negative charges and travel up to the cloud on the path of the leader. This return of positive charges is the main stroke of lightning. What we see as lightning travels upward is the *return stroke*.

Damage has been reported as the direct result of lightning. Fires have been started, trees have been scorched or struck down, buildings have been destroyed, and people have been struck and killed. Lightning rods are used on buildings and cars drag chains or straps to lead the charges into the ground where they become harmless.

Label the diagram.

2.21   Complete the labeling at the right side of the illustration. Four words are missing.

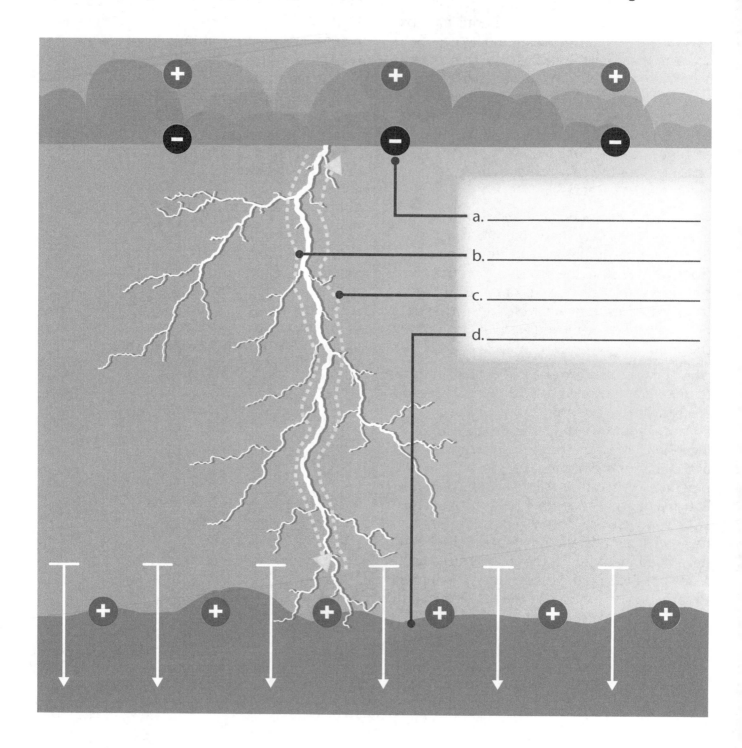

a. _____

b. _____

c. _____

d. _____

| Principle of Lightning

Answer these questions. Review Science LIFEPAC 806 if you need to

2.22 What are the two principles upon which static electricity and lightning are based?

a. _____ b. _____

2.23 How and why does static electricity move? _____

_____

2.24 What three precautions should you take during an electrical storm?

a. _____

b. _____

c. _____

2.25 Is a car a safe place during a lightning display? a. _____ Why or why not?

b. _____

Current electricity. Students ask "What is electricity?" as if it were a thing. Since it does not have size, shape, form, or substance, electricity cannot be described as an object. Look back at past discussions in your Science LIFEPACs, and you will notice that we are talking about how electricity *behaves.* The use to which we put electricity depends on its behavior. A light bulb is not electricity, but it becomes useful when electricity flows through it and gives us light.

Current electricity is produced when free electrons move through conductors. A *conductor* allows the electrons to flow. Metals are conductors because they have a large number of free electrons. Silver, gold, copper, and aluminum are the best conductors. They are used in homes and industry as electrical wires. Silver and gold are not practical conductors because of their high cost. Copper wire is more expensive than aluminum but has been the safest and most effective substance for practical purposes.

Have you ever wondered why building fires are investigated so carefully? The authorities are looking for the cause of the fire to determine

if a criminal act has taken place; have highly inflammable substances been stored illegally, was a faulty electric circuit installed, were building codes violated, or was a material used in building at fault? For a period of time in the 1970s, aluminum wiring was permitted for the branch circuits in homes. A number of serious fires occurred when the circuits became overheated. As a result, the use of aluminum wire for branch circuits has been discontinued, but it is commonly and safely used for feeder wires if it is properly installed.

Blackouts. Electricity is one of our most valuable assets. Homes and industry have become very dependent on electric power. A blackout (no electricity) **disrupts** our lives and threatens us with unexpected dangers. In 1965 the failure of an electrical relay in a hydroelectric plant in Canada started a chain reaction that blacked out Ontario, Canada, and areas of the northeastern United States including New York City. The relay was about the size of a small microwave oven and plunged 30 million people into a state of helplessness. The blackout lasted for fourteen hours. After this disaster, the power company took action to put many safety features into the system. New York City was separated from the rest of the area as corrections were made. The authorities said such a massive blackout would never happen again.

On July 13, 1977, it did happen again. The day was very hot, and the use of air conditioners and other cooling devices overtaxed the electrical system. No electricity was available for twenty-five hours. Not only was living without electricity difficult, but the darkness also encouraged vandalism, looting, stealing, starting of fires, and other crimes. Business and property losses climbed to the $1 billion mark. Thousands of persons were arrested. People who were not well, especially those with heart problems, had their lives threatened by inconveniences. Many high-rise buildings in big cities are used for offices, stores, businesses, and apartments. Elevators and escalators did not work. Subways and commuter trains were stalled. Gasoline pumps could not operate; consequently, cars, buses, and trucks could not get fuel. Water pumps stopped working. Toilets could not be flushed, and garbage disposals did not work. Food in refrigerators and freezers spoiled. Computers stopped and jammed the reservation systems for hotels, airlines, and trains. Hospitals are equipped with emergency generator systems and work to fill the needs partially, but not completely. Can you understand how disastrous a blackout can be?

Have you ever discussed an emergency plan with your family in the event electricity is cut off? Now may be a good time to do it. The New York City incident makes us aware of how dependent we are on the use of electricity. We have discussed only the uses that are obvious. Add to the list the thousands of indirect uses, and our dependence becomes even greater.

 Complete these activities.

2.26 The loss of electricity actually creates major catastrophe in the big city and disaster in less congested areas. List six ways the loss of electricity directly affected people in New York City.

Example: People in hotels with electronic locks on the doors could not get into their rooms.

a. _____

b. _____

c. _____

d. _____

e. _____

f. _____

2.27 List three ways people in rural areas can be affected by the loss of electricity.

a. _____

b. _____

c. _____

2.28 How could you alter your life style so that the loss of electricity would be something you could live with comfortably? Write a paragraph describing how you and your family could adjust.

_____

_____

_____

_____

_____

TEACHER CHECK _____ _____
initials   date

Sources of electricity. From where does the electric current come? Chemical and physical energy are changed to electricity. Volta discovered in the early nineteenth century that if a strip of copper and a strip of zinc are placed in a solution of sulfuric acid, a current of electricity is produced. The dry ends of the zinc and copper were attached to the light fixture with wire.

Volta guessed correctly that a chemical change was taking place that produced an electrical force, which we now call _electromotive force_. Electrons accumulate on the zinc strip, making it negative.

| A Wet Cell

| Dry Cell (cutaway view)

Electrons are lost from the copper strip, making it positive during the chemical change. If a wire is connected so that it makes a path, the electrons will travel through the wire from the zinc to the copper strip as a current. The electric light bulb was connected in the path and was lit by the current. For about one hundred years, electromotive force was the main source of current. Today's batteries and dry cells are the result of Volta's discovery.

Carrying sulfuric acid about is not practical. The dry cell, which is similar to Volta's wet cell, was developed. Ask your teacher if a cutaway dry cell is available so you can study it with this drawing.

A carbon rod is used instead of copper. The paste used is sal ammoniac, zinc chloride, graphite, and manganese dioxide. The container is the zinc.

The dry cell is a convenient source of electricity because it is easily moved about and does not use large, awkward equipment. Electricity produced by the dry cell and battery are small amounts compared to what a generator can furnish. An early term for the generator was the *dynamo,* which relates to the Greek word *dynamis* meaning *power.* The generator converts physical energy to electric current and makes it useful in large amounts. The powerhouses at the base of both the Hoover Dam and Niagara Falls contain turbines that revolve rapidly as moving water is directed at the turbine blades. The turbine is connected to the armature of the generator on which a coil is wound. The coil turns between the two strong magnets of the generator to produce an electric current. Physical energy is converted to electricity that can be used immediately. Electricity can travel at the speed of light, 186,000 miles per second.

This is a list of scientists who made valuable discoveries leading to modern-day electrical usage. Write their most important discovery. You may refer to Science LIFEPACs 806 and 810, an online resource, an encyclopedia, or other reference.

2.29   Robert J. Van de Graaff _____

_____

2.30   Joseph Henry _____

_____

2.31   Michael Faraday _____

_____

2.32   William Sturgeon _____

_____

2.33   Hans Christian Oersted _____

2.34   Alessandro Volta _____

_____

2.35   Luigi Galvani _____

_____

Sources of energy. The United States has been accused of being a **materialistic** nation. We use and enjoy the conveniences available to us. We have a good supply of coal, but burning coal produces dirt and gases. **Environmentalists** worry that this dirt and gas are destroying the air quality. We have adequate sun, wind, tides, and falling water, but our sources of oil and gas are running out. We must develop other energy sources and prepare for the future. Other countries are watching to see if Americans are willing to conserve energy.

Solar energy, geothermal energy, and nuclear energy are being developed. Researchers are working frantically to find ways of obtaining more oil and minerals from under the sea and the ice caps.

We depend on science to develop new ways to provide for the needs of the world. People look at all the advantages science technology has provided for them and conclude that the scientific way is basic to their life style and comfort. Great importance is placed on science and technology. Chemists, physicists, and engineers, their assistants, helpers, laboratory workers, and many others are guaranteed a future in science and technology. We need to learn to adapt to the changes science and technology can bring us. We need to meet the needs of the population.

We can learn from the animals who live on different kinds of food. If they lived on only one type of food and that food source disappeared, they would die. They learn to adapt. The resilience of our society would increase if other sources of energy were developed and used on a large scale. We could be more resilient if we took Joseph's advice. He told King Pharaoh to create storage in a time of plenty to be used in a time of scarcity. Read Genesis chapters 40 and 41.

God used Joseph, who then helped Pharaoh plan for his future needs. Through helping Egyptians, Joseph helped his own people. Only by God's power could Joseph foretell what would happen. If God accomplishes something through you, remain as humble as Joseph did. The people praised Joseph for his wisdom in preparing for the famine. He said (Genesis 41:16) "...It is not in me: God shall give Pharaoh an answer of peace."

 Complete this activity.

2.36 Write a 250-word report on one of the following topics. Write on a separate piece of paper. You may use an online resource, an encyclopedia, or some other reference for information. Check with your teacher about reading your report to the class. Your teacher will evaluate your paper first.

   a. Energy crises

   b. Energy conservation

   c. New sources of energy

   d. Influence of environmentalist on energy development

   e. Air pollution

   f. Aerosols and ozone

TEACHER CHECK _____ _____

                                              initials   date

MACHINES AT WORK

Energy occurs in large quantities in various forms such as mechanical, chemical, heat, and nuclear energy. Energy is defined as the capacity or ability to do work. Humans have found ways to use energy in machines to work for them. Machines make work easier and permit work to be accomplished that mankind could not otherwise do.

Work. The scientific meaning of work is *force multiplied by distance*. The word is used in many ways but always suggests that action has been accomplished. Your friend suggests playing ball after school but you say "Sorry, I have to do my mathematics." He replies, "Don't work too hard." Is that work? Not in the way the physicist considers work, but by definition it is *mental activity to accomplish something*.

Machines do much of the work accomplished. In underdeveloped countries where unemployment is very high, people are hired to do heavy work by hand. Stone and bricks are carried by men and women at construction sites. Foundations are dug with shovels. Hope for progress and advancement for these countries depends on providing machines.

You have seen many machines at work without probably realizing it. Machines lift, push, pull, and dig. They roll, cut, transport, twist, and straighten. In the playground, they are used for slides, swings, and balances. Machines help us solve problems by doing difficult work. At times we cannot accomplish work because the force (weight) is too great for us to move. The simple machines help us to do work and often are combined to make a complex machine such as the automobile. The basic machines work for one of three purposes: to *increase force*, to *increase speed*, or *to change the direction of the force*.

If a child lifts an adult by using a lever, the child is increasing their force. Beating egg whites to make them thick and frothy for the top of a lemon pie is difficult without an egg beater. The hand cannot move fast enough to get air into the egg white. Examine an egg beater. Notice the set of gears. The big gear turns once while the small one turns approximately five times. The direction of the force is changed to give five times as much force.

A beam extends from the top of the second floor of most barns. Hay is stored in the loft, but the farmer would not be able to get it there without help. A simple pulley is fastened to the end of the beam. By passing a rope over the pulley, one person can pull the bale of hay up to the loft while the other pulls it in and piles it in the loft. The direction of the force has been changed.

Try this investigation:

These supplies are needed:

- string
- books or blocks of wood
- spring scale
- board 2- to 3-ft. long (or a wood ramp)
- piece of metal or similar objects of different weight

Follow these directions and answer the questions. Put a check in the box when each step is completed.

☐ 1. Tie a piece of string around the object to be tested. Keep the string short. Weigh the item with a spring balance.

☐ 2. Rest the board on a stack of books making an inclined plane 1-foot high.

☐ 3. Pull the weight up the inclined plane with the spring balance. Find how much force is being used by reading the scale.

2.37 Is the reading on the scale ½ (for a two-foot board) or ⅓ (for a three-foot board) as much as the weight of the object moved? _____ If not, repeat steps one and two, and check again. Remember that some loss will result from friction.

2.38 What does mechanical advantage mean? _____

_____

2.39 What is the mechanical advantage of the inclined plane? _____

_____

2.40 What does the number in 2.39 mean? _____

_____

☐ 4. Repeat this investigation with a longer board and use objects of different weight. Raise the height of the inclined plane.

Inclined Plane Experiment

Friction: harmful or helpful. Rubbing your hands together in cold weather warms them. Moving parts of machinery are oiled or greased so that they will move with the least amount of difficulty. Native Americans used large stones to grind corn. After much use, the stones lost their shape and became smooth or hollowed out. In the first illustration, rubbing is helpful; in the last it is harmful. The use of oil or grease as **lubricants** on machinery reduces the friction.

The rubbing that generates heat and wear is caused by the resistance of the surfaces of the objects and is called *friction*. At one time people thought friction was caused by bumping and tearing of irregular surfaces. Increased knowledge about atomic structure shows us that friction is partly a result of the attraction of molecules on surfaces rubbing against each other. This attraction, called **adhesion**, can also be observed when liquids cling to the inside of jars or cans.

To overcome the harmful effects of friction, lubricants are used. They smooth the surface and prevent wear or make it possible to do work otherwise impossible. Oil, grease, petroleum jelly, soap, wax, and graphite are lubricants. Certain lubricants are better for specific jobs. A careful choice is important. Does your father use a certain kind of oil in the motor of his auto? Is oil or grease used to pack the wheel bearings?

Complete these statements by indicating what lubricant you would use in each instance.

2.41 The squeaky hinge of a door needs _____ .

2.42 Your ring is too small. You cannot take it off. Use _____ .

2.43 A window slides up and down with difficulty. Use _____ .

2.44 Wheels on the child's wagon squeak and are stiff. Use _____ .

2.45 A sewing machine needs _____ to work well.

Friction is also useful. A car has difficulty getting started on ice. Sand under the tires or the tread of snow tires gives more friction and enables the car to get going. Rubber mats and carpeting aid in walking on ramps. Brakes on a car work on the principle of friction. Tennis shoes provide better friction on a slick basketball floor.

Complete this activity.

2.46 Write a 250-word story describing what you think a day in your life would be like without friction. Read your story to a classmate, then give it to the teacher.

TEACHER CHECK _____ _____
initials   date

SIMPLE MACHINES

Mechanical advantage is increased by using a simple machine or a combination of them. The six simple machines include the lever, inclined plane, wedge, pulley, screw, and wheel and axle. Machines do not make energy, but use the energy provided them. The functions of the machines are to increase force, to increase speed, or to change direction of the force.

The inclined plane, pulley, screw, and windlass were used before the time of Christ. The Hebrews built the treasure cities in Egypt for the new king. Rock carved from the mountains was brought great distances to build the cities. The weight was too great for the men to lift. Rocks were dragged and pushed along the ground and up ramps. Pulleys of some form were probably also used as winches. In several places, the Bible speaks about water *drawn* from the well. The windlass was probably used to draw water in this manner. The wheel is not one of the simple machines but is used as a part of some of them. Evidence of the invention and use of the basic machines is found in the Bible. Pictures and drawings of ancient civilizations, especially Egypt, show the use of machines.

Levers. Levers are in everyday use. A board, a stick, or a metal rod can easily be used as a lever. The three classes of levers are best identified by the positions of *the resistance force*, *the effort*, and *the fulcrum*. The object to be moved is the resistance force, or load, the force applied is the effort, and the fulcrum is the point of balance.

With the first-class lever, the fulcrum is between the load and the effort. The wheelbarrow is a second-class lever. The wheel is the fulcrum, the load is in the center, and the effort is at the handles. The lower arm is a third-class lever. The hand holds the load, the bicep muscle pulls the arm up at the center of the lower arm, and the elbow is the fulcrum.

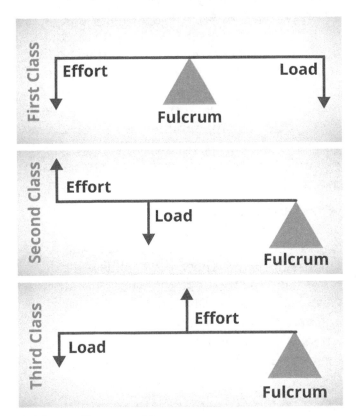

| Three Classes of Levers

The lever is in equilibrium, or balanced, when the effort multiplied by its distance to the fulcrum is equal to the resistance force multiplied by its distance to the fulcrum. The effort multiplied by its distance to the fulcrum is called the *torque*. The same is true for the resistance force. When in balance, the effort torque and the resistance torque are equal except for loss due to friction.

Inclined plane. The inclined plane is represented by the ramp. A greater distance is covered, but the effort needed to move the resistance is less. A 50-gallon drum of a chemical weighs 160 pounds. A 12-foot plank is placed from the ground to the bed of the truck. The ramp is three feet high. Rolling the barrel up the plank and into the truck is four times as far as the distance the barrel is to be lifted. The effort required is only ¼ the weight of the barrel, or 40 pounds.

Pulleys. Single pulleys provide an easy way to lift and lower loads. The single pulley lifts hay into the barn, moves the flag up and down the pole, and lifts sails on a mast. The single pulley is useful because the weight of the body aids in pulling the rope. A *compound pulley* is a series of pulleys. Compound pulleys increase force. A man using a compound pulley must move a greater distance, but he will use less force. For example, a fixed-movable pulley system has a mechanical advantage of 2.

Wheel and axle. A wheel and axle gains force at the expense of distance. A screwdriver as it is used for turning a screw is a wheel and axle. The handle is the wheel, the shaft is the axle. A doorknob is the rim of the wheel. Rotate the knob and the axle will act to turn the mechanism of the door. If you do not think the wheel is helpful, loosen the screw and remove the doorknob. Try to turn the axle with your fingers.

Wheels equipped with teeth that mesh are gear wheels and are mounted on axles. Gears are used to increase speed, to increase force, and to change direction of the force. The eggbeater is a familiar example of a gear that increases the speed of the force and changes the direction of force.

Wedge. The wedge is a double inclined plane. The main use of the wedge is to split or to separate an object. If the wedge is 2 inches wide and eight inches long, it will penetrate a log to a depth of eight inches and will split it 2 inches. The ratio 8:2, or 4:1, is the mechanical advantage (M.A.) If 400 pounds of force is needed to split the log, an exertion of 100 pounds will be used.

Screw. A screw is really a curled inclined plane. Cut a piece of paper into a right angle triangle with the hypotenuse, 8⅜ inches: the base, 7¾ inches; and the height, 3⅛ inches. Starting with the 3⅛ -inch side against the pencil, wind it around the pencil, keeping the base line even. The hypotenuse, an inclined plane, resembles the thread of the screw. The screw is used in two simple machines: the wheel and axle and the inclined plane. A wrench turning a bolt is an example. The wrench handle and head of the bolt are the wheel and axle and the thread of the bolt is the screw. A car jack or a house jack are good examples. The jack is a bolt with a screw head to which the handle is attached. The bolt fits into a nut, which is the base. The load to be lifted rests on the screw head. As the handle (the wheel and axle) is moved, the screw turns out of the base and lifts the load. The load is moving up the inclined plane of the screw. Houses and cars can be lifted by this technique. The M.A. of one simple machine is multiplied by the other. Combined advantage can be very large. A small amount of advantage is lost to friction.

Humans were restrained by the limits of their own strength when all they had to work with was their own muscles. Not until they learned to use machines could they take advantage of the power available to them in wind and water.

Write true or false.

2.47 _____ Machines have been used for thousands of years.

2.48 _____ The Bible gives no evidence of simple machines.

2.49 _____ The wheel was the first simple machine invented.

2.50 _____ Some mechanical advantage is lost to friction.

2.51 _____ Graphite helps overcome friction.

Make these drawings.

2.52 Draw the three classes of levers labeling the resistance load, the effort, and the fulcrum. Show the direction of force of the resistance and effort for each one with arrows.

    a. First-class lever   b. Second-class lever   c. Third-class lever

2.53 Draw a pulley with a mechanical advantage of 2.

2.54 Draw an inclined plane with a 200-pound load being moved a height of 4 feet up a 16-foot ramp. Label the drawing and show amount of effort used. Solve for the effort by finding mechanical advantage.

    a. Drawing   b. Mathematics

TEACHER CHECK _____ _____

                                         initials   date

Review the material in this section in preparation for the Self Test. This Self Test will check your mastery of this particular section as well as your knowledge of the previous section.

SELF TEST 2

Match these items (each answer, 2 points).

2.01	_____	km/h	a.	100
2.02	_____	centimeter	b.	kg
2.03	_____	energy at rest	c.	1/1000
2.04	_____	hecto	d.	electrons
2.05	_____	distance × force	e.	10
2.06	_____	kilogram	f.	speed
2.07	_____	sawdust + salt + iron filings	g.	potential
2.08	_____	in orbits	h.	cm
2.09	_____	dekagram	i.	mixture
2.010	_____	milligram	j.	work
			k.	compound

Write the letter of the correct answer in each blank (each answer, 2 points).

2.011 The lowest temperature humankind has not reached is called _____ .
a. Fahrenheit b. absolute zero
c. kinetic energy d. Celsius

2.012 Heat is transferred from one object to another by _____ .
a. expanding b. energy c. radiation d. oxide

2.013 Alcohol ($2C_2H_6O$) has _____ atoms of hydrogen.
a. 2 b. 12 c. 4 d. 6

2.014 Magnetism penetrates _____ .
a. steel b. Alnico c. iron d. glass

2.015 When a current flows through a wire, a(n) _____ surrounds the wire.
a. field of force b. electromagnet c. current of air d. power

Complete these statements (each answer, 3 points).

2.016 Machines are used to increase a. _____ , increase b. _____ , and/or c. _____ .

2.017 Some mechanical advantage is lost to _____ .

2.018 AMA is a. _____ and IMA is b. _____ .

2.019 Mechanical advantage equals a. _____ divided by b. _____ .

2.020 Chemical change takes place when a. _____ and b. _____ change.

Define these terms (each answer, 5 points).

2.021 alloy _____

_____

_____

_____

2.022 lubricant _____

_____

_____

_____

2.023 convection _____

_____

_____

_____

60/75   SCORE _____   TEACHER _____ _____

initials   date

3. LIFE SCIENCE

The Bible states (1 Corinthians 3:16 and 17), "Know ye not that ye are the temple of God, and that the Spirit of God dwelleth in you? If any man defile the temple of God, him shall God destroy; for the temple of God is holy, which temple ye are." The *temple* in the Bible refers to God's house, the place where God dwells and where people worship. As Jesus ascended into heaven, he promised a *power* would come to live in His people to take His place. They were to wait. Christians stayed in Jerusalem until the Holy Spirit descended upon them and came to live in them. The Christian today is the temple where the Holy Spirit lives.

This section is part of the study of living things and deals with the growth and care of the human body. Accept the scientific principles of nutrition and good health, and pay attention to recommendations made by authorities. Your body, the temple of God, will then be pleasing to God.

The body is similar to a complex machine. The working parts perform in a complicated way that is difficult for humans to understand. We know that if we give the body the right fuel (food) it will run and produce energy through chemical and physical change. The human body operates at a high rate of efficiency; it uses 90 percent of its fuel with 10 percent waste products. Machinery needs proper fuel and good care. The human body requires the same attention.

SECTION OBJECTIVES

Review these objectives. When you have completed this section, you should be able to:

11. Explain how the human body functions like a machine.
12. Tell how we must care for our body as the "temple of God."
13. List job opportunities in the life sciences.
14. Describe the balance and disruption of nature and state your place in the universe.

VOCABULARY

Study these words to enhance your learning success in this section.

alimentary (al' u men' tur ē). Connected with food and nutrition.

autonomic (ô tu nom' ik). Any process that occurs without thinking; automatic.

essential (u sen' shul). Absolutely necessary.

nutrients (nü' trē untz). Nourishing ingredients in a food.

peer (pir). A person of the same age and status.

regulate (reg' yu lāt). To control or direct according to rule or principle.

NUTRITION

The food you eat today and tomorrow will affect what you will be in the future. *Nutrition* is the science of eating a proper balanced diet to promote good health. In this section we shall consider what the body needs, how the body digests food, and what plan (diet) you should follow.

Six kinds of nutrients. The body has a remarkable way of selecting what **nutrients** it needs from the foods you eat. The problem is to give the body foods from which it can take what you need. A walk through the supermarket makes one aware of the vast variety of foods available. A knowledge of the kinds of foods needed by the body will enable one to secure a balance of nutritious foods to stay healthy. Six **essential** food nutrients must be a part of a daily diet. They are fats, carbohydrates, proteins, minerals, vitamins, and water.

Carbohydrates are a *fuel* food for the body. Carbohydrates are mainly composed of starch and sugar. The chemical structure of starch and sugar is similar. During the process of digestion, they are changed to glucose as they produce energy. *Fats* and *oils* are the second group of fuel foods. When fats are oxidized during digestion, they produce about twice as much energy as carbohydrates.

Water, minerals, and *proteins* are needed for building the body and keeping body parts working. Two-thirds of the human body is water that is taken in directly and that is present in most foods. Minerals are only needed in small amounts, but they are essential to the body. Bones need *calcium* and *phosphorus* for growth; the blood must have *iron* for hemoglobin; the thyroid gland needs iodine; fluoride prevents tooth decay; and much more. *Proteins* are for growth, cell replacement, and the production of enzymes and hormones. Since they resemble body protein, they are found mainly in animal products.

Vitamins are found in small quantities in most foods. They **regulate** the chemical activity and growth of the body.

Digestion. The **alimentary** canal is a very complicated organ that does a difficult job. The process of digestion is automatic since it is controlled by the **autonomic** nervous system. Our concern is to give our body the food it needs.

A simple description of the alimentary canal is that it is a flexible, muscular tube lined with mucus, glands, and cells that produce chemical substances. The chemical substances act on the food and break it down for absorption into the body. Science LIFEPAC 804 contains further details of the digestive system.

The muscular tube which is the digestive system has walls containing smooth muscles. The unusual arrangement of the muscle fibers gives the tubes the ability to contract. The partially dissolved food is moved through the tract bit by bit by a process called *peristalsis*. About 90 percent of the food is digested and can pass through the walls of the intestine into the bloodstream. The blood then carries the nutrients to where they are needed.

Complete the sentences. Review Science LIFEPAC 804 if you need to.

3.1   The body is _____ water.

3.2   In the digestive process food is _____ changed.

3.3   In the digestive system food is broken down by _____ .

3.4   Food moves through the digestive system by the muscular action called

_____ .

3.5   The digestive system is controlled by the _____ system.

Diet. A good diet supplies all the nutrients the body needs for growth and repair. A proper diet should provide an adequate amount of water. Water is necessary to keep blood flowing and digestion moving. We need water to stay alive. The autonomic feeling of thirst is our body's way of telling us that we need water. Many foods have high water content, especially fruits and vegetables. Drinking approximately eight glasses a day should be plenty of water for good health.

The necessary nutrients are found in foods. To be certain you are getting what your body needs, you should include food in proper quantities from different food groups.

The diet referred to here is the general diet that furnishes the body with fuel. Usually the word diet refers to special diets for special needs such as overweight, underweight, or illness.

Complete this activity.

Write what you had to eat yesterday, placing it in one of these categories. If you do not know whether a specific food is nutritious or junk food, you may use an online resource, an encyclopedia, or other reference.

3.6   nutrient foods _____

_____

3.7   junk foods _____

_____

Answer this question.

3.8   Do you think your diet was good yesterday? a. _____

Explain your answer. b. _____

_____

HEALTH

Poor eating habits are injurious to health. Foods are often glamorized by attractive packaging and by deceptive advertising, but foods that appear delicious might not be very nutritious.

Nutritional diseases. Nutritional diseases are the result of poor nutrition through bad eating habits, poverty, famine, ignorance, and deliberate use of harmful substances. Digestion and other body processes are affected by poor diet. Some people believe that all illness is related to nutrition. This statement seems to be exaggerated, but diet is the first thing regulated for any illness treated in a hospital. The dietitian is a very important member of the hospital staff.

Junk foods are defined as substances with very low nutrient content. Salt and sugar are the most common ingredients in junk food. Books on food fads and diets are often on best seller lists, kept there by people who are badly informed and seek something unusual. Food faddists are motivated by ignorance or money or both.

Additives are hidden criminals in our diet. The law states that every chemical used in food processing must serve one or more of the following purposes:

1. Improve nutritional value.

2. Enhance quality or consumer acceptability.

3. Improve the keeping quality.

4. Make the food more readily available.

5. Facilitate its preparation.

Most food additives have nothing to do with nutritional value. People are surrounded by pictures of beautiful foods and expect to have them that way. Vegetables from the fields are dirty. Fruits are not as pretty as the consumer wants them to be. Pesticides, fungicides, and other spoilants are used on them. Oranges are often dull, therefore they are dyed with orange-colored chemical.

Additives include preservatives. Some of these chemical preservatives have been proved scientifically to cause damage to human beings. Many school children have difficulty learning and are too active to sit to learn. This condition has been improved by removing additives from their diet. Cancer is caused by some additives but may take twenty years to develop. Problems caused by additives are difficult to identify. One should try to learn what additives to avoid.

 Answer these questions.

3.9   If additives and junk foods are dangerous, what can you do to protect yourself?

_____

3.10   Study the five points of the law on additives. Answer these questions.

  a. What is basically wrong with the law?

_____

  b. How much would you change the law to get better protection?

_____

_____

Deficiencies, allergies, and other reactions. Problems that are a result of poor nutrition seem to prove that illness can be caused by what you eat. These diseases are not normal and are found in areas of poverty, overpopulation, and famine. People in the United States do not always get these diseases, but they sometimes have the symptoms.

Medical help is available and specialists are able to correct those problems. If you are troubled by an allergy or deficiency, you may be interested in reading more about it. To maintain good general health in terms of nutrition, one should learn what foods are in each nutrition group and should eat a well-balanced diet.

 Complete this activity.

3.11 Explain what you can do to maintain good general health in terms of nutrition.

_____

_____

Hygiene. Hygiene is defined as the science of health and its maintenance. Hygiene is dependent on a system of principles for the preservation of health and prevention of disease. It includes any rules you have learned about nutrition, the prevention of disease, and the personal care of your body.

The body is the temple of God to be cared for and watched over faithfully and with caution. Personal care includes knowing about good nutrition, paying attention to all the rules of cleanliness of the body and mind, and not exposing the body needlessly to disease or to harmful foods, drugs, or eating habits.

Young people are eager to be accepted by their **peers**. Sometimes young people decide to follow the wrong leader. Results may be harmful. Life is a total period of growth; but during the earlier years character is formed, habits for the future are established, and conditions of mind and body are fixed. Personal hygiene means to follow all principles for preservation of health, not just personal cleanliness. Make the right decisions now!

Match these items.

3.12	_____ temple of God	a.	following health preservation principles
3.13	_____ total period of growth	b.	developed early in life
3.14	_____ person of same age	c.	includes good nutrition, cleanliness, and avoidance of harmful foods and drugs
3.15	_____ science of health		
3.16	_____ personal hygiene	d.	results may be harmful
3.17	_____ character and habits	e.	peer
3.18	_____ personal care	f.	life
3.19	_____ following the wrong leader	g.	your body
		h.	prevention
		i.	hygiene

BALANCE IN NATURE

Orderliness is evident in all areas of scientific investigation of the universe. Photosynthesis is an extraordinary function of plants. Basic materials necessary for plants and food supplies for all living things in the earth are produced by this function. Photosynthesis also returns oxygen to the air.

Photosynthesis. Photosynthesis is a very complex process. Science LIFEPAC 809 contains a detailed explanation of the process. Green plants combine atoms from carbon dioxide and water to form sugar and oxygen. This complex process is made up of a series of complicated steps that occur when sunlight and chlorophyll are present. This chemical equation is a summary of all the steps:

$$6\ CO_2 + 12\ H_2O \rightarrow C_6H_{12}O_6 + 6\ H_2O + 6\ O_2$$

Radioisotopes are an important by-product of atomic energy research. Isotopes give off various amounts of radiation without additional stimulation. Radioisotopes are used as tracers or spies to study living things. New information has been made available on scientific processes not formerly understood. Radioactive carbon dioxide has been used as a tracer to study photosynthesis. A recent important discovery is that the oxygen that becomes part of the sugar molecule comes from the carbon dioxide (CO_2) and not from the water in photosynthesis.

Complete this activity.

3.20 Put the chemical equation for photosynthesis, $6\ CO_2 + 12\ H_2O \rightarrow C_6H_{12}O_6 + 6\ H_2O + 6\ O_2$, into a statement using words and numbers.

_____

_____

_____

Natural cycles. As a food is produced and consumed, chemical changes are taking place. Elements in the soil are used and need to be replaced. Respiration of animals uses oxygen and produces carbon dioxide. A process in plants requires carbon dioxide and produces oxygen. Similar cycles involve water and the decay of plants and animals. These cycles are in balance except when humans interfere and add to the entropy of the universe.

Nitrogen cycle. Nitrogen is a major element needed for plant growth. The atmosphere cannot provide it in a free state. Bacteria aid in fixing the nitrogen in soil. The _Rhizobium_ bacteria live in the nodule of the root of the plants known as legumes. Clover, beans, peas, alfalfa, and peanuts are legumes. The bacteria consume the sugar and starches of the plant and convert nitrogen found in the soil into compounds the plant can use. Surplus nitrogen is returned to the soil.

Legumes are plants frequently used for crop rotation. They restore the soil's nitrogen that has been taken from the soil by the previous crop. Nitrogen is an animal waste product of protein consumption. Amino acids are removed from the body by urea. When this substance reaches the soil it returns nitrogen. Decayed animals and plants return nitrogen. Fertilizers and _Rhizobium_ bacteria may both be applied to the soil to increase nitrogen content.

 Make a drawing.

3.21 Draw a diagram representing the nitrogen cycle. Label the parts.

Water cycle. The human body is two-thirds water. The earth is three-fourths water. Water evaporates from the surface of bodies of water and is a product of the respiration of animals and transpiration of plants. As the atmosphere becomes heavy with water molecules, clouds are formed. The clouds become saturated with moisture that returns to the earth as precipitation in the form of rain, snow, hail, or sleet. The water is again available to animals and plants.

 Make a drawing.

3.22   Draw a diagram showing the water cycle. Label the parts.

Carbon-oxygen cycle. Carbon and oxygen are discussed together because they are so closely related. Plants use carbon dioxide and release oxygen by means of photosynthesis. Animals use the oxygen and release carbon dioxide as a waste product of respiration. The aquarium is a miniature world that demonstrates the carbon-oxygen cycle under water.

 Make a drawing.

3.23   Draw a diagram of the carbon-oxygen cycle. Label the parts.

Decay cycle. The progression of life on earth ends in death for plants and animals. Decay follows death. Chemical changes with the help of bacteria return dead plants and animals to the soil as elements much needed to maintain a balance of food. Food is sometimes too plentiful and must be disposed of. Tons of fruit and vegetables are plowed into the ground each year. Animals are disposed of by burial. They decay to return elements to the soil. Chemicals are frequently used to speed the decomposition.

 Make a drawing.

3.24 Draw a diagram of the decay cycle. Label the parts.

Balance and disruption. Each cycle has been shown as the ideal way to keep nature in balance. God created the heavens and the earth in perfect balance. Humankind's disruption of the environment has changed the natural balance and has destroyed animals and plants from microorganisms to huge redwood trees.

Some results of the advanced civilization have been mechanization and the continuation of wars, greed, and selfishness. Forests have been destroyed by fire and used recklessly to provide buildings and other products for human comfort.

Animals have been destroyed by hunting and fishing and the greed of those who killed for fur, meat, ivory tusks, and other body parts. Water and air have been polluted by industrial wastes.

Conservation groups are active in fighting the wasteful use of natural resources. Animals almost extinct are gradually increasing their numbers. Laws have and are being passed to save animals and plant life and to control the pollution of air and water.

Complete these statements.

3.25 The cycles found in nature are created by _____ .

3.26 All the cycles working together bring about a(n) _____ in nature.

3.27 Disruptions in nature are caused by _____ .

3.28 Some of the disruption can be halted by a. _____ and

b. _____ .

JOBS AVAILABLE IN HEALTH SERVICES

God created the world as a perfect unit, but humans cause destruction. Sin came into the world and with it pain, sickness, unhappiness, war, and other problems. The remedy is Jesus Christ who died to save us from this sin and to give us a new life and a new heart. Christians are drawn to jobs where they can help others. There are countless job titles in the health services field, and there is a wide range of positions and skill-sets that fall into this category. Workers in health services have the ability to help people each day and demonstrate Jesus' love.

The following list shows jobs in health services:

- Therapy and Rehabilitation occupations
- Occupational Therapists and Physical Therapists
- Speech Pathologists and Audiologists
- Medical Assistants and Aides
- Dietitians
- Pharmacists
- Opticians
- Physicians and other types of doctors
- Nurses
- Hospital and Medical Record Administrators

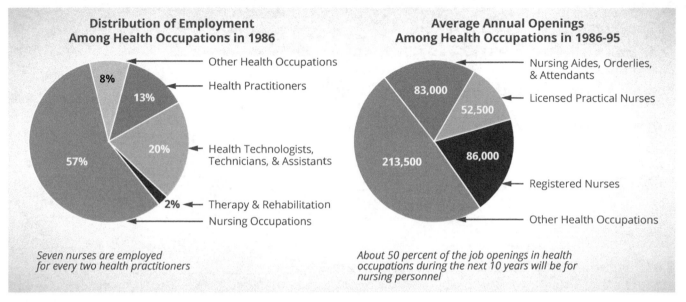

Figure 7 | Health Services 1986   Figure 8 | Health Services 1990s

 Do this activity.

3.29   Choose a health service career in which you are interested. Write a 200-word report on the
            career that you have chosen. Include such information as the amount of education it requires,
            the kind of work it involves, the number of opportunities in the field, and so on. You may use
            the library to gather information about a specific career or you may talk with someone who
            already works in the career field you are interested in. Show your report to your teacher.

TEACHER CHECK _____ _____
                           initials   date

Review the material in this section in preparation for the Self Test. This Self Test will check
your mastery of this particular section as well as your knowledge of all previous sections.

SELF TEST 3

Complete these sentences (each answer, 3 points).

3.01 If the body is given the right food, it will produce energy through a. _____ and b. _____ change.

3.02 The six kinds of nutrients are a. _____ , b. _____ , c. _____ , d. _____ , e. _____ , and f. _____ .

3.03 Another name for the digestive system is the _____ canal.

Write true or false (each answer, 1 point).

3.04 _____ Fats produce twice as much energy as carbohydrates.

3.05 _____ Whatever food you eat, you should take vitamins.

3.06 _____ Digestion is under your control.

3.07 _____ The blood carries nutrients to where they are needed.

3.08 _____ A good diet is only a part of what the body needs for growth.

3.09 _____ Corn, wheat, and tomatoes are legumes.

3.010 _____ Personal care includes knowledge of good nutrition.

3.011 _____ Without photosynthesis we would have no food.

Match these terms (each answer, 2 points).

3.012 _____ green color in plants   a. balance in nature

3.013 _____ $C_6H_{12}O_6$ b. photosynthesis

3.014 _____ radioisotope   c. entropy

3.015 _____ nitrogen cycle   d. legumes

3.016 _____ destruction in universe   e. conservation

3.017 _____ organized   f. chlorophyll

3.018 _____ control of fishing   g. tracers

3.019 _____ nitrogen producers   h. orderliness

     i. sugar

Answer these questions (each answer, 5 points).

3.020 How does the body resemble a machine?

_____

_____

_____

3.021 How do people *defile* their bodies—God's temple?

_____

_____

Make a drawing (5 points).

3.022 Draw and label a diagram of the water cycle.

Complete these items (each answer, 5 points).

3.023 Name and describe the three methods of heat transfer.

_____

_____

_____

3.024 Explain the process of electrolysis.

_____

_____

61 / 76   SCORE _____   TEACHER _____ _____
                                              initials   date

4. VOCATIONS IN SCIENCE AND TECHNOLOGY

Your education has been general up to this point. The foundation has been laid in basic skills and in general information. High school is a good time to consider specialization. If you plan with thought, you will save yourself valuable time. After the first year in high school, you will have choices.

Think now about the career(s) you want to know more about. Science is very promising. Read about it and study the **prospects**. Libraries have books, pamphlets, and encyclopedias on careers. Survey what they have and add to this outline on how to prepare yourself. Seek God's will for your life (read Proverbs 3:5 and 6).

SECTION OBJECTIVES

Review these objectives. When you have completed this section, you should be able to:

15. Describe vocational opportunities in science and technology.

16. Develop techniques for working out a career plan.

VOCABULARY

Study these words to enhance your learning success in this section.

prospects (pros' pekts). Looking forward to something; likely candidates.

résumé (rez' u mā). Summing up; statement of a job applicant's background.

sedentary (sed' un ter ē). Keeping one seated much of the time.

TECHNOLOGY TODAY AND TOMORROW

Statistics show that technology is an expanding field of study. As humans try to improve the quality of their lives, they find more and more ways to use the scientific findings of pure science. Most of the uses have been beneficial, but very often they are available to only a few people. There is much poverty on the earth, and many people have little or no food to eat. In other areas food is plentiful. Medical availability is in limited supply to poor people all over the world. Our use of technology is hampered by the growth of industry and government. People could be served better if technology were more manageable. United States citizens have great advantages in the way they live, eat, and are able to obtain medical help. If severe storms occur, however, power is wiped out, roads are blocked, food is unavailable, hospitals are out of reach, and electric equipment is unworkable. We have not conquered weather or such physical catastrophes as earthquakes. We also cannot ignore human error.

Today. You have learned many of the basic principles of science. You have explored the smallest particle of matter. You have investigated living things, including the human body. To think about all you will do in your future science studies with more complicated equipment is exciting. When you learn science principles or work to formulate principles, you are practicing pure science. Some of you have used science kits and equipment, such as microscopes or telescopes, at home. You enjoyed the experience and you think that you would like to be a chemist, physicist, physiologist, astronomer, or a research scientist.

What are the interests expressed by most of your classmates? Do they talk about being a doctor, farmer, astronaut, nurse, mechanic, dietitian, or engineer? If they do, they are more interested in technology than in pure science. A successful career in science or technology requires study, practice, and application.

We are reminded in the Bible to study, to work, and not be idle or lazy. If you think this effort is too much, remember the rewards. Just as God punishes for sin and provided a Savior, Jesus Christ, to rescue us from punishment, the Bible gives us many instructions and commands that seem hard to follow. However, God knows it is not easy for us and gives us strength if we ask Him. He promises us gifts. In Ecclesiastes 12:12 God says that much study makes us tired; but chapter 3, verse 13 of the same book says that we should enjoy the good of all our work because it is God's gift.

Tomorrow. The job market is competitive, especially for young adults. The United States Department of Labor reports that only 60% of young adults between the ages of 20 and 24 were employed in 2020. Additionally, 41% of recent college graduates have jobs that do not require a college degree, meaning that they were not able to find a job in their field (2019). The number of workers with college degrees is going up faster than the number of jobs they would prefer. Technology is opening a wide range of jobs that will improve opportunities for every well-trained worker. The best-educated work force this country has ever had will be waiting to make its contribution during the next twenty years. Will you be ready?

In general, the greatest number of jobs available will be in technology and health services. However, there are other categories included in the projections for the fastest growing and most available jobs, including positions that do not require a college education.

Table I will give you information about current occupation growth and the projections for the next ten years. You will most likely be looking for a job in less than ten years. Now is the time to think about your high school curriculum and what subjects you should take. Your first task is to select your area of interest, or several areas, and to consider your abilities. The following table is a partial list showing growth and decline.

Occupation	Opportunity			
	Excellent	**Very Good**	**Fair**	**Declining**
Registered Nurse	X			
Cooks, Food Service	X	X		
Software Developer	X			
Electrician			X	

Occupation	Opportunity			
	Excellent	**Very Good**	**Fair**	**Declining**
Construction			X	
Agriculture				X
Nurse Practitioner		X		
Laborer		X		
Financial Manager		X		
Federal Government				X
Information Security Analyst	X			
Artist				X
Therapist (occupational, physical, etc.)	X			
Secretary and Administrative Assistants				X
Marketing	X			
Teacher			X	

Table I | Occupation Growth 2019 and projected 2029

 Complete these activities.

4.1 Ask five of your classmates, boys and girls, what vocation they would like to follow and add your choice to the list. List the jobs on the chart and place checks as appropriate. Reference employment projections posted by the U.S. Bureau of Labor Statistics (https://www.bls.gov/) or other sources online.

Job for (name)	Projected Growth	Projected Decline	Education Needed	Average Salary
	Excellent	**Very Good**	**Fair**	**Declining**
Example: Social Worker Jane	X		Bachelor's or Masters	50,000

TEACHER CHECK _____ _____
                         initials   date

✎ **Complete these statements.**

4.2 A large number of positions will be available in _____ related areas.

4.3 God tells us to not be a. _____ or b. _____ .

4.4 Although God's commands are stern, He promises _____ .

4.5 List four technology or health related jobs that you might like and are good possibilities for your future. You may reference information online (labor statistics) to make your choices.

_____

_____

Learn this scripture.

4.6 Write Ecclesiastes 3:13 in the space provided.

_____

_____

_____

ASSETS AND LIABILITIES

Evaluate yourself for your good points (assets) and those things that should be changed (liabilities).

Tests. Tests as evaluators help you judge yourself. Tests have been given you since you started school. Enlist your teacher's help as to your strong and weak points. Accept advice. Special interest tests mean selecting areas of interest to you. Civil service examinations, college entrance examinations, and tests for special colleges and vocational schools such as art school, technological schools, medical laboratory training, business college, driving heavy equipment school, and others are special interest tests.

Tests can be classified as:

1. *Maximum performance tests* – work as hard as you can to get as many right as possible. Tests academic skills, specific abilities, or how much you learned in school.

2. *Nonacademic tests* – United States Employment Service tests that measure general reasoning, form perception, vocabulary, arithmetic skills, clerical aptitude, motor coordination, and finger dexterity.

3. *Company tests* – some companies have their own test to measure the kind of aptitude they need.

4. *Personality tests* – to measure personality and interests.

Experience. However young you are, doing a job well will teach you good work habits. The jobs your parents give you or cutting grass for the neighbors are good experience. Volunteer work is available to young people.

Training. Accept instructions from your employer and follow them even if you think your way is better. You have to please your employer, and you can always learn something new.

Character. A good character is your most valuable possession. You are the only one who can control your character. If Jesus is your partner and you listen to His guidance through His Word you will be the best.

Likes and dislikes. Narrow down your career possibilities.

1. Indoors or outdoors; active job or **sedentary**?
2. How much education should you have?
3. Work with people or work alone?
4. Is a job helping others or is money your goal?
5. Are you listening for God's call to His work if this job is His will?

 Answer these questions.

4.7 What does sedentary mean? _____

4.8 What is your most valuable possession? _____

4.9 What are tests called that measure personality and interests? _____

4.10 What are nonacademic tests? _____

_____

4.11 Why should a person your age get a job? _____

_____

FINDING A JOB

Eventually, you will be seeking a job that will begin your career. Consider the following ideas to prepare yourself.

Good work habits. A habit is something that develops over a period of time. A habit becomes a part of you. Work on developing good habits from now on.

1. Be dependable.
2. Be efficient.
3. Use initiative.
4. Be honest.
5. Be pleasant and friendly.
6. Be courteous.
7. Be neat.
8. Develop good health habits.

Have a development program. Each person should have a plan to develop their own talents and use them to God's glory. Plan your development program early.

1. Getting job experience is part of a development program.
2. Keep reading and learning.
3. Learn to like people and get along with them.
4. Work on personal skills such as speech, behavior, and emotional control.
5. Check your appearance regularly.
6. Obtain a social security card as required by law.

How to look for a job. Looking for a job is very important. The first impression you will make will be a lasting one. Remember, you are God's representative.

1. Know about the job you are seeking.
2. Write a **résumé** for yourself and take it with you when you go job hunting.
3. Know how to fill out an application blank. Be truthful!
4. Check your appearance before going in for an interview.
5. Know how to act during an interview. Do not wiggle or chew gum.
6. Call back after a reasonable time.

Where to look for a job. Knowing where to look for a job can save you much time and energy. Several sources are good places to start. Then follow through.

1. Relatives and friends may be able to help you.
2. Use connections in the workforce and contacts with former employers.
3. Employment agencies will help people over age 18.
4. Know how to write a cover letter and résumé.
5. Check legal age limits for jobs.
6. Search online job postings and generate leads through social media.

Write a résumé.

4.12 An employer will be very impressed if you can produce a résumé when you are asked to make out an application. Your résumé should include your name, address, age, telephone number; education; training; previous employment; extracurricular activities; applicable skills and hobbies; three character references with names, addresses, phone numbers. When you are an adult, your resume will include different information.

Write a résumé in an orderly fashion that you would be pleased to show an employer. Double-check spelling. Do this activity on a separate piece of paper and turn it in to your teacher.

TEACHER CHECK _____ _____
                                          initials   date

↺ **Before you take this last Self Test, you may want to do one or more of these self checks.**

1. _____ Read the objectives. See if you can do them.

2. _____ Restudy the material related to any objectives that you cannot do.

3. _____ Use the **SQ3R** study procedure to review the material:

   a. **S**can the sections.

   b. **Q**uestion yourself.

   c. **R**ead to answer your questions.

   d. **R**ecite the answers to yourself.

   e. **R**eview areas you did not understand.

4. _____ Review all vocabulary, activities, and Self Tests, writing a correct answer for every wrong answer.

SELF TEST 4

Match these terms (each answer, 2 points).

4.01	_____ greatest number of jobs	a.	special school
4.02	_____ found in molecules	b.	lubricant
4.03	_____ personal inventory	c.	tests
4.04	_____ an asset	d.	clerical
4.05	_____ evaluation	e.	work
4.06	_____ special interest test	f.	iron
4.07	_____ oil or grease	g.	good character
4.08	_____ distance times force	h.	résumé
4.09	_____ hemoglobin	i.	atom
4.010	_____ art school	j.	civil service exam
		k.	application

Complete these statements (each answer, 3 points).

4.011 To aim for a happy career, consider your a. _____ and

b. _____ .

4.012 When seeking a job bring your _____ with you.

4.013 Energy at rest is said to be a. _____ and energy in motion is

said to be b. _____ .

4.014 Like poles of a magnet _____ each other.

4.015 To work, you are required by law to have a(n) _____ .

Complete this list (each answer, 3 points).

4.016 List five elements of good character.

a. _____   b. _____

c. _____   d. _____

e. _____

Complete these items (each answer, 5 points).

4.017 Write Ecclesiastes 3:13 in the space provided.

_____

_____

_____

4.018 Explain how the metric system might affect your adult life or career.

_____

_____

_____

_____

4.019 Explain the difference between a mixture and a compound.

_____

_____

_____

_____

Match the item in each set (each answer, 2 points).

4.020 _____ water stored behind a dam   a. potential energy

4.021 _____ water in a cloud   b. kinetic energy

4.022 _____ moving vehicle

4.023 _____ falling rock

4.024 _____ charged storage battery

· ·

4.025 _____ digestion   a. physical change

4.026 _____ photosynthesis   b. chemical change

4.027 _____ melting ice   c. nuclear change

4.028 _____ atomic reactor

· ·

4.029 _____ ax head   a. lever

4.030 _____ system to raise flag on a pole   b. wheel and axle

4.031 _____ screw driver turning a screw   c. inclined plane

4.032 _____ rear wheel of ten-speed bicycle   d. screw

4.033 _____ ramp   e. wedge

4.034 _____ claws of a hammer   f. pulley

                                              g. gear

· ·

4.035 _____ legumes, bacteria, clover   a. water

4.036 _____ carbon dioxide, breathing, photosynthesis   b. carbon and oxygen

4.037 _____ evaporation, lakes, condensation, rain   c. decay

                                              d. nitrogen

Before taking the LIFEPAC Test, you may want to do one or more of these self checks.

1. _____ Read the objectives. See if you can do them.
2. _____ Restudy the material related to any objectives that you cannot do.
3. _____ Use the **SQ3R** study procedure to review the material.
4. _____ Review activities, Self Tests, and LIFEPAC vocabulary words.
5. _____ Restudy areas of weakness indicated by the last Self Test.